108

B.

1948.

QUEEN OF TO-MORROW

A charming studio portrait of the Princess taken not long before her engagement.

Queen of To-morrow

An Authentic Study of
H.R.H. The Princess Elizabeth

By

LOUIS WULFF, M.V.O.

author of
"Elizabeth and Philip"
and
"Silver Wedding"

LONDON
SAMPSON LOW, MARSTON & CO., LTD.

The Princess enjoys nothing more than reading in the quiet comfort of her own apartments. Note the walnut tallboy, the firescreen with the Royal Arms, the dial telephone, and the carnations.

Acknowledgment is made for the black and white illustrations in this book to the following :—

New York Times Photos—London

P.A.—Reuter Photos.

The Times.

International News Photos.

Graphic Photo Union.

Fox Photos Ltd.

Planet News Ltd.

Central Press Photos Ltd.

The "Topical" Press Agency Ltd.

Photo Illustrations, Scotland.

A. V. Swaebe, London.

"Harlip" London.

The Associated Press Ltd.

Keystone Press Agency Ltd.

Harris's Picture Agency.

Studio Lisa.

Dorothy Wilding, London.

Marcus Adams.

London News Agency Photos Ltd.

Photographic News Agency Ltd.

Photograph by Baron.

Ministry of Information, Crown Copyright Reserved.

Made and printed in Great Britain by Purnell and Sons, Limited
Paulton (Somerset) and London

Author's Foreword

IN THE two years which have passed since the first publication of this book, Princess Elizabeth has firmly established herself as the recognised leader of the youth of Britain and the Empire. Her conscientiousness in the performance of her public duties, the noble ideals she has put forward in her speeches and broadcasts, have won her world-wide respect and admiration. In the British Commonwealth, she is loved not only for the high qualities that so well become her as Heiress Presumptive, but for herself, in her own person, with an affection that transcends all party and political differences. Her love-match and happy marriage sent a gleam of happiness across a sad and disillusioned world. Men and women of many different creeds rejoice that the future destiny of the British Crown should be in the hands of one who has so clearly shown herself worthy in every way of the high standards and selfless traditions that adorn the Throne. When, on her twenty-first birthday, she made a dedication of her life to the service of the people of our Imperial family, she called on the people to join with her in her resolution, and her clear young voice, heard in all the capitals of the Empire as she spoke from Cape Town, tied another of those tenuous, steel-strong, impalpable bonds which hold Britain and her sister nations together in free association, pointed the way to a future of mutual service and support. To-day, the Empire centres round the person of His Majesty the King. On some to-morrow, Princess Elizabeth will take his place, and her whole life forms an omen of good for the Empire's morrow.

L. W.

East Horsley,
July, 1948.

One of the most charming of her early portraits. On her grandmother's knee, the baby Princess smiles. She wears her first necklace of corals.

Contents

QUEEN OF TO-MORROW

First Edition November 1946
New Impression May 1947
Second Edition October 1948

An informal, happy picture of Princess Elizabeth and her husband off-duty. Side by side, they sit watching a cricket match on the Royal ground in Windsor Great Park, just as thousands of other couples throughout the length and breadth of England like to sit on a Sunday afternoon. Royal cares are put aside, as the Duke of Edinburgh, who has just made seventeen runs, watches his side batting.

CHAPTER ONE

Princess of To-day

CHARM is a quality which eludes definition. Throughout the ages, poets, orators, and writers have attempted to tabulate its ingredients, but none has completely succeeded. It remains the quality which all men and women want to possess, but which it is impossible to acquire by lesson or striving. So when a Frenchman, well experienced in the ways of the world, remarked, after following Princess Elizabeth during her four-day visit to Paris, that he could best account for the extraordinary impression she had made on the people of the sophisticated French capital by the simple statement: "Elle a du charme", he was saying at the same time both everything and nothing: everything because without that charm which we have come to know as part of her the Princess could not have won the Parisians' hearts: nothing because his words go no further towards explaining the secret of her attraction.

Many others of high and low degree, from Ambassadors to factory hands, have attempted, like that Frenchman, to account for the effect the Princess produces, without any conscious effort, on the crowds wherever she goes. None of them has come any closer to an explanation. The simple fact is that her Royal Highness the Princess Elizabeth, heiress presumptive to the British Throne, is a young woman who has such natural grace, such a pleasing personality that even were she not in her exalted station, she would still command the affection and respect of all who met her.

This is a circumstance of much greater import than would at first appear, for on the personality of this young woman of twenty-two much depends to-day and much more may well depend in the future. She is heiress to the greatest inheritance and the heaviest responsibilities in the world. Almost alone amid the wrecks of thrones broken during the cataclysm of the world struggle, the Throne of the British Commonwealth of Nations remains as firm if not firmer to-day than ever. The occupant of that Throne is the wearer of the imperial crown, whose twenty-inch circle of gold stretches to span the world. Sharing common ideals, the love of freedom, hatred of oppression, desiring to live and work in peace with fair shares for all, the nations of the British Commonwealth have no other legal tie than their common allegiance to their mutual Sovereign.

Therefore it is on the personality of the occupant of the Throne that the thoughts and aspirations of men and women all over the world are focused, for it is not only by the Sovereign's official acts, but by the mode of his own private life, that he moulds and guides the destinies of millions of his subjects.

From the very moment of her birth at 2.40 in the morning of April 21, 1926, Princess Elizabeth Alexandra Mary Windsor has been, with gradually increasing intentness, trained as the future occupant of the Throne. When her uncle, the Duke of Windsor, abdicated after his brief reign as King Edward VIII the destiny that fate had marked out for her became more clear. With the accession of her father as King George VI

"*Capped and Gowned.*" *Princess Elizabeth, Mus. Bac. smiles after receiving her honorary degree at London University.*

She chooses a "*New Look*" *umbrella in a smart tartan.*

on December 11, 1936, she became, and remains to-day, Heiress Presumptive to the Throne. It is indeed a good fortune and a blessing for the British people that the young woman thus exalted to so high a pinnacle has already proved herself so worthy and so fitting in every way to occupy it.

In the four years that have elapsed since Princess Elizabeth became of royal age on her eighteenth birthday, she has gained the love and affection of many thousands of men and women in all stations of life, all over England, Scotland, Wales and Northern Ireland, throughout the Union of South Africa and in both the Rhodesias, and most recently in France. Few people could be found to deny that she is the most popular, as well as the best known woman of her age in the world to-day. Such a position is a dangerous as well as a difficult one. It would be easy for its holder to come to regard the plaudits of the multitude as her natural right, to assume that people must naturally be pleased to see her. No such thoughts have ever come to Princess Elizabeth. She shows, with that same natural sincerity of expression that is one of the Queen's most endearing characteristics, that she is always delighted, and even a little surprised, at the warmth of the welcome and the depth of affection with which she is greeted. Her life, even in our modern world where austerity forcibly levels so much of the existence of all into a dull grey monotone, is necessarily apart from the existence of most of her contemporaries. The black and gold railings outside Buckingham Palace keep not only the crowds away from the grey stone Palace buildings, but represent the intangible barrier which must exist between Royalty and their subjects.

PRINCESS OF TO-DAY

Such barriers are an integral part of the conception of monarchy. They do not and cannot exist in a republic. It is unthinkable, for example, that the King's housekeeper should publish a "diary of Buckingham Palace", and the private lives of members of the British Royal Family are, by general agreement, safe from intrusion. With a wisdom beyond her years, Princess Elizabeth has found an ability to cross that barrier, to put herself in touch with the lives of the people outside the gates of her father's Palace without losing any of her Royal dignity. She is well aware of the concepts and ideas that find place in the minds of her father's subjects. She has a deeper insight than many politicians into the feelings of the men and women who on such occasions as her own wedding day crowd in scores of thousands around the Palace, cheering and calling to see her and her family.

It is by their public speeches, both in their substance and in the manner of their delivery, that Royal personages are best known to the general public, particularly in these days when the microphone brings their actual words and the inflections of their voices to the ears of all. Few people who have heard Princess Elizabeth making a speech have failed to be impressed by her candour and wholeheartedness. What she says she obviously means, and she has a way of saying it in simple words that reach directly to the hearts of her hearers. She takes immense care in the advance preparation of her speeches, sparing, as it is to be expected, no pains to acquaint herself fully with the subject in hand. But it is in her felicitous choice of phrases that the Princess most shines. With an intuitive sense of words, she has a habit of substituting such phrases as "my father and mother" for the formal "their Majesties the King and Queen", which make her speeches an expression of her own personality. That personality is a subject which interests not only the heads of foreign missions accredited to her father's court but countless millions of ordinary folk all over the British Empire, the United States and in many other parts of the world.

" That's where we were on your wedding day, ma'am." Captain Collyer of the New Zealand barque Pamir *shows the Princess and the Duke the position on a chart.*

QUEEN OF TO-MORROW

Her greatest beauty is in the near perfection of her natural English colouring. Her eyes are deep blue, luminous and intelligent. It is taking no poetic licence to describe her complexion as cream and roses, and it owes nothing to art. She has a graceful figure and moves with ease and dignity.

She has beautiful white, evenly spaced teeth, which give brilliance to her smile, so strikingly reminiscent of her mother's. Her hands are small and shapely. Yet the secret of the Princess's charm does not lie here, though her natural physical attraction is part, and an important part, of her personality. None of the Princess's photographs, in colour or in black and white, do her full justice. This is not only because even the best of photographers, working with the most modern of colour equipment, cannot hope to reproduce in exact value the delicate tints of her fair complexion and exquisite colouring, but also because the radiance of lively happiness that emanates from her can never be captured by the camera. It is no infrequent experience, to those travelling behind Princess Elizabeth as she tours the crowd-packed streets of some provincial town, to hear repeated cries of "Oh, but she's beautiful!" The men and women in the crowds say this in some surprise, as if taken a little unaware to find her so much surpassing their expectations. One secret of her charm lies in the fact that she is a very happy person, with the same unconcealed delight in life, the same intense and eager interest in all that goes on around her, as the Queen. Princess Elizabeth never looks bored, in her pictures or in life, and this is not the result of Royal training—though it is one of the occasionally more difficult obligations of Royalty to avoid showing their feelings in public,

The Royal smile that is world famous: Princess Elizabeth in a smart hat and a happy mood.

no matter how long or how tedious the programme arranged for them may be, —but springs from her real sense of the freshness of life, her constant interest in people and their varied activities.

Another factor that contributes greatly to her charm is her unaffected naturalness. She does not, as so many lesser people do, keep one character for private life, and another to don, like a mask, in public. In the centre of the stage at some big public function, receiving the freedom of one of her father's cities, or lending her invaluable anxiously-sought support to some cause for the public good, or in the privacy of her own home, she is just the same. She owes little to art, either in her way of speaking or in her outward appearance. Her voice, clear and well-modulated, is unaltered, save in strength, whether she is making a speech or talking to friends, the expression in her clear, direct eyes is nearly always friendly. Though she is a believer in the modern way of life, with its greater freedom for young folk, she has no time for those who take things to extremes. Nor does she favour artificiality in any way. Her use, or rather her non-use, of make-up is an indication of this facet of her character. In daytime, Princess Elizabeth uses almost no cosmetics, save for a little powder and the minimum of lipstick, and for evening parties she uses little more.

Vivid lipstick, rouge, eyeblack, brilliantly coloured nail varnish, none of these makes any appeal to the Princess. In a Mayfair ballroom she is often among the least conspicuous, as well as the most attractive, young women present. One of her dislikes, of which there are quite a few, is for exaggeration or over-elaboration whether in appearance, in adornment, or in art, which is one of the essential first foundations of good taste.

Her good taste in artistic matters is a quality of which those outside Court circles have only recently become aware. When Princess Elizabeth, following in the footsteps of her great-great-grandfather, Albert the Prince Consort, became President of the Society of Arts in 1947, she went to the Society's headquarters in John Adam Street, Adelphi, to deliver her inaugural address. Some number of the rather elderly, distinguished Council members

As Colonel of the Grenadier Guards, she frequently inspects men of her regiment.

A Dominion handshake: she greets a lady from Pakistan.

had met her before, but for most of them it was their first meeting with the young Heiress Presumptive. They, together with the members of the Society who packed the lecture hall when the Princess rose to speak, were most interested in their new President, and in the manner in which she would acquit herself, but they had no great anticipation that what she would say would be of anything more than formal interest. After the Princess had uttered her first few sentences, however, a new air of real interest in her words was apparent. She was not merely uttering a series of formal platitudes but venturing to express her own opinions on art, much as her great-great-grandfather used to do. She spoke openly and strongly of her conviction that beauty must not be overlooked in industrial design, suggested that manufacturers would do well to consult artists when planning their products, and remarked that in an austere age it was for us to establish beauty as an essential to utility.

"It may be long years before we can again afford to devote such leisure and energy as our forefathers did to things purely decorative," said the Princess. "But we should be defeatist indeed if we conclude that because nearly everything we produce to-day must be severely practical it must also be without taste or beauty. A nation whose level of good sense in art was once reflected in the furniture of Chippendale and Hepplewhite and in the domestic architecture of the eighteenth and early nineteenth centuries cannot rest content with slavish imitations of foreign styles or with a simple faith in the virtues of streamlining. Great Britain led the world into the industrial revolution. There had been a legacy of squalor, misery and ugliness as well as the fall in standards of taste which accompanied mass production. In a sense we have a duty to lead the world in finding the remedy."

This was the first occasion, apart from her twenty-first birthday broadcast, when the Princess had introduced a really serious note into a speech.

The applause when she sat down was sincere as she has ever received, for she had put into words, and plain words at that, what nearly all of her hearers were thinking. Now, they felt, a new Royal champion of the arts had arisen, and a rare blush of deep pleasure mantled the Princess's cheeks as she received the congratulations of the Council. Deep though her feelings on such subjects may be, the Princess knows too much and has her actions under too strict control to permit herself to embark on an over-vigorous campaign for art in industry. She is conscious of her own youth and comparative inexperience, realising that she must make her point gradually, and that to assume over-suddenly the role of an arbiter of elegance would be merely to diminish, perhaps to destroy, the influence she is anxious to exert.

Her concern with the preparations for the centenary of the Great Exhibition of 1851 is another pointer to her interests in this direction. So, too, are the words she used at Coventry, when she opened the new spacious Broadgate planned to take the place of the crowded shops and cramped streets that Hitler's bombers demolished.

Speaking of the re-building of bombed areas, she said, "Our generation has many responsibilities. First, in the bombed areas we must be sure that the style and the materials we use are of the highest quality we can devise. We have a glorious tradition in architecture, but in the last hundred years we have not always lived up to it."

In her own life, the Princess has no place for second-best. She believes that the same policy must be of benefit to the country generally. What she believes to be good she already has little hesitation in preaching in her speeches. In future as she gains in experience and influence, she will continue to say, with more emphasis, what she feels to be right, adding the strong encouragement of her own example to the strength of her words, for she is a young woman of great strength of character, not easily swayed or diverted from her purpose, as she has already shown several times and in several ways. Her adventure on VE night when she went out with Princess Margaret into the thick of the victory crowds around the Palace, accompanied only by two police officers in plain-clothes, is already history: to it, she has added many other examples of her tenacity of purpose, and disregard of strict precedent.

Always, in this direction, she must be ruled by the principal edict of our constitutional monarchy: to avoid any reference to political questions. But outside the sphere of political argument, there are hosts of matters on which the Princess can, and will, give a lead to the nation. High among these is the cause of stamping out cruelty to children. Nothing has given her greater horror than recent cases of this which have come before

With her grandmother, Queen Mary, the Princess goes to see her pink diamond, a wedding gift from Tanganyika, being cut in Clerkenwell.

An experience which was to become familiar: the Princess rehearses her first broadcast, while Princess Margaret looks on.

the courts, and she takes her work as President of the National Society for the Prevention of Cruelty to Children with very great seriousness.

Brought up for the first sixteen years of her life in careful seclusion from the public, Princess Elizabeth was, in many ways, young for her years when she came of age. It says much both for her character and her training that the transition from that early life of happy privacy into the full glare of publicity that follows almost every movement of the Heiress to the Throne has affected her scarcely at all, except to make her more conscious of her high responsibilities. Poise is a quality that is hers by grace of nature. It enables her not only to accomplish such difficult but minor feats as retaining her dignity and controlling her skirt when climbing out of an aeroplane, but also on a higher plane to accept the loving adulation of the multitudes without losing her simplicity or becoming spoilt. Gay by nature, fond of fun, high-spirited and always ready for laughter, the Princess is nevertheless a person of serious mind. The key to her actions to-day is to be found in the solemn words of dedication she spoke in her twenty-first birthday broadcast from Cape Town, a broadcast that was the twentieth-century version of the ancient religious avowal of their lives to chivalry by the Kings and Princes of old.

"I declare before you all that my whole life, whether it be long or short, shall be devoted to your service, and the service of our great Imperial family to which we all belong, but I shall not have strength to carry out this resolution alone, unless you join in it with me, as I now invite you to do," said the Princess.

Princess Elizabeth and Princess Margaret enjoy the morning sun on the Castle lawns at Windsor, where they spent most of the war years. Between them is Dookie, one of their pet Corgi terriers.

Photograph: Studio Lisa.

PRINCESS OF TO-DAY

With an absence of stilted phrases or high-flown hyperbole, she made her vows in the simple direct words that carry more weight because they come from the heart. Since that April day in South Africa, Princess Elizabeth has kept her high purpose of service to others always in front of her. Her coat-of-arms bears no motto. Were she to adopt one, none could be found more apt than the words "I Serve"—which so many of her ancestors wrote beneath their crests as "Ich Dien".

The crimson and gold trappings of State, the pageantry that is part of monarchy, seem ill-suited to these present grey days of scarcity and shortage. It is because the British Royal family have been able to transmute that gold of ceremony into the plain but strong steel of service that the monarchy stands in such universal high regard to-day. In that continuing alchemy of an ancient institution, Princess Elizabeth plays a major part. It is a task for which she is well fitted both by nature and by training. She has never suffered from that shyness which made every public appearance an ordeal for her father in his young days. Though her education was planned on lines which deprived her of the companionship and competition of other girls of her own age whom she would have met in the schoolroom or the college lecture hall, the Queen encouraged her friendships with other girls, with the "children next door"—the son and daughter of Lord and Lady Allendale, who lived in the next house to 145 Piccadilly, Princess Elizabeth's girlhood home, the private house which the King has referred to as the "Palace with a Number". She was not allowed to feel the isolation from the world that has bred so much introspective unhappiness among princes, and the sad remark attributed to Queen Wilhelmina of the Netherlands when as a little girl she scolded her dolls with

The Princess stands godmother at the christening of the baby of a close friend.

17

Against a background of rondavels in the Kruger National Park, South Africa.

The King and his daughter enjoy a joke: a happy moment during the South African tour.

the threat that if they did not behave they would grow up into princesses and have no one to play with, would never have been comprehensible to her.

Marriage has added, as happy marriage does to all women, to the Princess's stature. She has a warmer, more mature outlook to-day than she had in those days when all the world was speculating whom she would marry, and when.

As a young married woman, the Princess has shared with many of her future subjects an experience that has fallen the lot of few Princesses in history. She and the Duke of Edinburgh have had no London home of their own for the first year of their married life. Like so many thousands of other newly-married couples of post-war days, they have had to live with parents, and though the Princess's parents are King and Queen of England, though their temporary home is a very comfortable flat in Buckingham Palace, where they can live their lives with complete freedom and independence, it is still not the same thing as having their own roof, a disadvantage that must be of profit to the Princess since it gives her an insight, however slight, into the lives of others less fortunate than she. Knowledge of the way other folk are living, an understanding of their problems and perplexities, are two essential attributes for royalty of to-day: and it is one of the restrictions of royalty that they can never, even in their off-duty hours, entirely ignore what other folk are thinking. The Princess and her husband had an early reminder of this after their official visit to Paris at Whitsun, 1948, when the small fact of their having visited a very innocuous night-club in one of the most respectable parts of Paris was construed by the narrow minds of certain chapel sects into a desecration of the Lord's Day, because it happened that the visit was made on a Sunday evening. No one with any pretentions to tolerance could see any possible harm in this very ordinary exploit, more particularly since the night-club in question was taken over in entirety for the occasion by the British Embassy in Paris, and only official guests were admitted. "A dark day in our history," was how one enlightened cleric chose to describe the occasion: and a dark day it was indeed if it gave re-birth to the sabbatarian intolerances of puritanism. But blameless though the Princess and the Duke were of any intention of hurting the feelings even of those who regard the ordained day of rest as a day on which no pleasure may be taken, they are unlikely to make a similar visit again on a Sunday, whatever their private feelings may be. Sunday observance in its extreme form is a matter of controversy and it is a tenet of the British Royal family to avoid all controversial issues.

That very minor incident serves to show how delicately royalty must tread, how many and how close are the restrictions on the lives of those who seem to have all made smooth and easy for them.

The Paris visit was the occasion for a display of the Princess's remarkable ability for retaining control of a situation well calculated to embarrass older and more experienced folk.

The main function on her programme was the opening of the exhibition of Eight Centuries of British Life in Paris, at which her speech in French was to be broadcast.

This was the first time the Princess had been abroad, the first time she had spoken in public in a foreign language. After lunching at the British Embassy in the Rue Faubourg St. Honoré, Princess Elizabeth and the Duke of Edinburgh drove with the Ambassador, Sir Oliver Harvey, to the Musée Galliéra where the exhibition was housed. A long flight of stone steps, lined by soldiers of the Garde Republicaine, faced the Princess and her husband, with two ornate chairs for them at the top, and a microphone between them,—not exactly the most reassuring of settings for the young Royal speaker. Up the several score steps the Princess walked with easy dignity, and took her seat to listen to the preliminary speeches. When she rose, in turn, to speak, a great burst of applause greeted her from the enthusiastic Parisians, whose hearts, always well-disposed towards an attractive woman, were utterly captured by the grace and natural charm of the Princess from across the sea. The applause died down, the

A wartime occasion: when the Princess launched H.M.S. Vanguard. *Mr. A. V. Alexander, then First Lord of the Admiralty, is at her side.*

Princess began to speak in her clear light voice that is so like her mother's, her French accent impeccable as always, with just a trace of nervousness in her tones as she gazed at the sea of faces beneath her, when another noise intruded itself. Bells in a near-by church began to ring. Thinking, perhaps, that this was a signal of welcome to her that had become a little delayed and would soon cease, the Princess carried on with her speech. But the bells continued, too, for they were ringing to celebrate a christening, and had no relation at all to the Royal programme. Before they had died down, another interruption came, this time in the form of a number of Press photographers, who suddenly appeared almost between the legs of the guard of honour, crouching on the steps in fantastic attitudes, and, with Gallic exuberance, letting off flash-lamps, though it was broad daylight. Besides all this, intermittently there came the whirr of cinema cameras recording the scene, a combination enough to put out any public speaker, however experienced. But Princess Elizabeth took the varied disturbances in her stride, smiled, and went on with her speech so calmly and so little moved that those listening to her by radio had no hint, save for the unexpected background of churchbells at the beginning, of the difficulties under which she was speaking.

It is by her perfect behaviour in trying circumstances like these that the Princess seals her popularity with all classes: and no British visitor to Paris since the days of Edward VII, that great lover of France and all her ways, has achieved a warmer place in French hearts than did his great-granddaughter, Princess Elizabeth, in the space of four short days.

That visit, designed simply to afford the Princess an opportunity of seeing Paris for the first time, had no political objectives. Yet it had political, or rather diplomatic, consequences. For the presence of the Heiress of the most stable monarchy in the world in their capital was not without its effect on Frenchmen inclined to doubt the stability of anything in the post-war world: nor did it fail to strengthen the already strong bonds between the two countries. One Paris paper of the extreme Left, for example, devoted three columns of its front page to a bitter attack on the British handling of the Palestine situation. Side by side with this article was a four-column lyrical account of the Princess's first day in Paris which would not have looked out of place in a French Monarchist publication. It is easy to exaggerate the lasting effect of a Royal visit like this, but many sage European diplomats considered that Princess Elizabeth and her husband, by their personal bearing and charm in Paris, helped the cause of Western Union at least one step forward.

Another hitherto unrecorded story of the French Royal visit throws a light on the character of the Duke of Edinburgh, and illustrates how real and deep is his affection for and interest in things of the sea. The night train conveying the Princess and her husband had not long come to rest aboard the ferry in Dover Harbour, when a tall figure in naval uniform climbed up to the bridge to greet the captain. It was Prince Philip, come up to see the ship taken out of harbour, that spectacle that never loses its fascination for a sea-lover, whether the ship be large or small. Once at sea, he went down again to his sleeper.

On that trip, the Princess had her husband with her. But the Duke's firm keenness on making a career for himself in the Navy involved them in a good deal of separation in the first year of their married life, while the Duke worked hard and assiduously at his

A typical gesture of friendly greeting: Princess Elizabeth acknowledges the cheers as she drives out of Buckingham Palace in an open landau.

In uniform, the Princess stands at attention with her father and her fiancé in honour of the dead: at the Cenotaph service, 1947.

studies at the Royal Naval Staff College. His uncle, Earl Mountbatten of Burma, left behind him in the Navy the unique record of coming out first in every examination he took. The Duke, not aspiring to emulate that wonderful performance, nevertheless determined to do justice to his heritage of the Mountbatten brains, and not to allow his studies to suffer by neglect. Accordingly, he refused all social engagements save for a few of the very highest priority, which meant that the Princess had to fulfil many engagements on her own. This involved some disappointment to the crowds who wanted to see their Princess's sailor husband, to say nothing of the Princess's own personal desires: but from childhood she has learned the Royal lesson of duty first, and the minor disappointment of the crowds was nothing compared to the criticism that might have been directed towards the Duke had he been content to abandon his own career, and take place merely as the Princess's consort. On her first visit to Oxford, and again at Cardiff, where she went to receive the freedom of the loyal Welsh City whose citizens, four years earlier, had bestowed on her their own title of "Ein Twysoges"—Our Own Princess—she had, to the general regret, to appear without the Duke.

PRINCESS OF TO-DAY

At Oxford, in the historic Sheldonian, where so many of the famous have been admitted to the academic roll of Oxford, the Princess, her young attraction set off by the bright red and deep crimson of her Doctor's gown, the flat black velvet cap of her degree on her light brown hair, received the honorary degree of Doctor of Common Law. It was her second degree, for already she had been admitted *honoris causa* to London University as a Bachelor of Music: and like the first it was a fitting degree for her. Constitutional history was one of her most deeply studied subjects, and she has, too, a considerable knowledge both of modern English law and of the old Roman code from which so much of it sprang.

There is, in the Sheldonian, when Convocation meets, an atmosphere that probably can be reproduced nowhere else in the world, as though all the spirits of the great, wise, and learned men of Oxford's past come to see who it is whom their successors deem meet to honour.

This time there certainly can have been no doubt in their minds, for all would agree with the mellifluous Latin in which the Public Orator, perched in his traditional semi-pulpit rostrum above and to the left of the Princess praised the new young Doctor. The legalistic form and much of the wording of the diploma which the Orator reads on these occasions are of considerable antiquity, varying little from that used when Dr. Johnson received the M.A. in 1755, but there were several personal references to Princess Elizabeth couched in those happy and apposite phrases which are to be expected from a University. After a reference to the cheerful acceptance by those of Royal stock of arduous tasks in peace and war, the Diploma (which the Princess now keeps among her personal papers) continues: "And, whereas Her Royal Highness the Princess Elizabeth Alexandra Mary has invoked from her earliest youth the motto of her House, in solemn dedication to the service of her country and having entered from her very girlhood upon the path of public duty, has earned by her queenly grace, her lively intelligence, and her charm of character such esteem at home and abroad as warrants in all men's sight, the highest hopes reposed in her." It would be difficult to improve on that succinct summary of the Princess's attainments. When it came to the turn of the Vice-Chancellor of the University to give the Princess her degree, he referred to her in the Latin phrase

With Mr. Winston Churchill, the Architect of Victory, in their midst, the Royal Family appear on the Palace Balcony on VE Day. Princess Elizabeth wears uniform as a subaltern of the A.T.S.

Princess Elizabeth, youngest Lady of the Most Noble Order of the Garter, and her husband, the Duke of Edinburgh, the youngest Knight, walk in their magnificent robes in the Royal procession from St. George's Chapel after the installation service at Windsor. Other Knights of the Garter and the heralds and officers of the College of Arms in their emblazoned tabards line the steps.

QUEEN OF TO-MORROW

"Principem Iuventutis", used in Imperial Rome to designate the Heir to the Empire, and thus an apt translation of Heiress Presumptive.

Besides receiving her degree, the Princess visited and walked round no fewer than eight Oxford Colleges that day, and it is typical of her that this long programme was the result of her own wish, not of any effort by the University authorities to take advantage of her presence among them. In fact, she twice sent draft programmes back to Oxford, asking that they should be extended to enable her to see more of the colleges.

That is one way in which Princess Elizabeth shows her Royal grace. Another Royal gift which she has inherited from her father and her grandmother, Queen Mary, is an extraordinary memory for faces and names. Not long ago, she went to an informal reception at Overseas House, St. James's, where hundreds of men and women from various parts of the Empire were assembled to receive her. With no prompting, and without hesitation, the Princess walked over to one woman,

In their plumed hats, and dark blue mantles, emblazoned with the badge of the Order: Princess Elizabeth, Lady of the Garter, and the Duke of Edinburgh, Knight of the Garter, after their installation at St. George's Chapel, Windsor.

and engaged her in earnest talk about South Africa and Australia. It was an Australian woman whom the Princess had last seen on the Royal tour in South Africa over a year earlier. Another example of this gift, so invaluable to Royalty, occurred at the Silver Wedding reception at Buckingham Palace, where the State Rooms were crowded with famous and notable figures. Again without prompting or hesitancy, the Princess went up to one of the men guests, greeted him by name, and talked over old times with him. He was a former member of the King's Household when he was Duke of York, and Princess Elizabeth had not seen him for at least eleven years,—just half her own lifetime.

With this, the Princess combines another Royal gift which adds greatly to her popularity wherever she goes. She never gives the appearance of neglecting anyone. With a crowd of bustling, over-anxious officials around her, she never allows herself to be in the least flurried, and should one keep her in conversation too long, she has the ability to turn easily away to greet some minor, less-important person waiting eagerly for Royal notice.

As she gains in experience, meeting more and more of the famous and distinguished, going more and more among her father's subjects of all classes, Princess Elizabeth has gained in stature and grace, without ever losing that fresh interest in all that goes on

26

around her which was one of the first qualities she showed in her early years. She is a young woman of very great natural intelligence, with a deep fund of common-sense which, edged and tempered by her wide reading, training and increasing experience, make her a person of wise outlook and balanced judgement, unlikely to be content to take things at their face value or to put up with shams. While it is true that she is still a very young woman, shrewd judges are confident that her personality is one of the strongest forces for good in the British Commonwealth to-day.

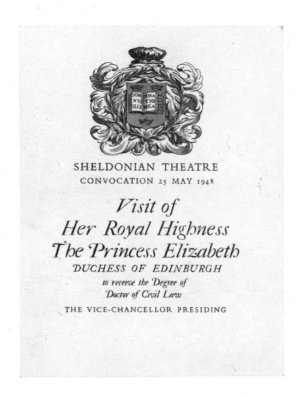

SHELDONIAN THEATRE
CONVOCATION 25 MAY 1948

Visit of
Her Royal Highness
The Princess Elizabeth
DUCHESS OF EDINBURGH
to receive the Degree of
Doctor of Civil Law
THE VICE-CHANCELLOR PRESIDING

Eleven years old, Princess Elizabeth takes dignified leave of the Bishop of London after an Empire Day service at Westminster Abbey, while Queen Mary watches.

CHAPTER TWO

The Training of a Twentieth-Century Princess

PRINCESS ELIZABETH'S training for the duties of Royalty began soon after she had learned to walk. Those first lessons were simple, intended to emphasise, almost unconsciously, with the utmost gentleness, the need for that extra courtesy, that little added touch of consideration for others that has come to be the first social duty of the British Royal family, something we are apt to take as much for granted as we do the courtesy of our police: but something which, again like police courtesy, does not always prevail in other countries.

Since then, her training has gone on with gradually increasing seriousness of purpose, has become more and more complex, wider in its scope, deeper in its implications, to fit her for the vastly complex and deeply significant part she is called on to play in world affairs. An apt and ready pupil in all manner of studies, as ready to learn from books as to gain knowledge from personal experience, the Princess has profited well from her training, until to-day she faces her high duties with the serene confidence that comes from thorough preparation. It was in the homely atmosphere of her nursery at Piccadilly, at her mother's knee, that the foundations of her great promise to-day were laid, as she learned in simple fashion from perhaps the most charming tutor in the land, the elementary lessons of obedience to God, response to duty, and thoughtfulness for others without which manners, however polished, and wits, however keen, are of little worth. It was from her mother, too, that the Princess learned the first great accomplishment of all, the lessons that are the corner stone of all learning: for it was the Queen who taught her daughter to read.

As she sees and rejoices in the success which the Princess everywhere attains to-day, the Queen may well feel a wholly justifiable pride in the results of her early training. Between the King and Queen and their daughters there exists as complete a mutual relationship of love, trust, understanding and sympathy as could be found throughout the King's dominions, a close-knit family affection that has its deep roots in those nursery days in Piccadilly, where first Elizabeth, then Margaret, were taught, by example and precept, the simple rules of family happiness. Probably at no time ever in the long story of the British monarchy has there existed such a perfect affection and understanding between the Sovereign and the heir to his throne. That particular relationship is agreed by all historians and philosophers to be one of unusual difficulty, calling for the exercise of the greatest tact and delicacy of feeling on either side, and there is no Royal House, including our own, whose record has not been marred by unseemly differences between the reigning monarch of the day and his next-in-succession. Queen Victoria's own early days on the throne were clouded in the reverse direction by antagonism with her mother: much later in her life, her inability to delegate authority to the eldest son with whom she never could manage to see eye to eye, helped to bring misunderstanding and unhappiness

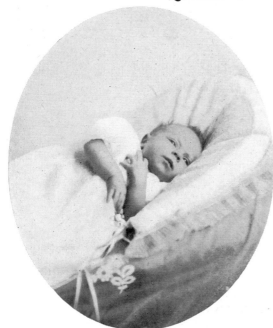

*The first picture of the most
photographed of Princesses.*

to both. Even in much more recent times, in the reign of King George V, the relationship between the King and Queen and the young Princes and their sister was much more formalised than was generally, perhaps, realised at the time outside the immediate Court circle. There was a distance between the King and his subjects, which even his own children could not entirely bridge, affectionate and dear as was his regard for each and all of them. Across that little distance, family familiarity was apt sometimes to remain a little strained. Princess Elizabeth and, for the last six years of his life, Princess Margaret, were exempt from this rather austere treatment. Between them and "Grandpa King" there were no barriers. So much did King George delight in the society of his granddaughter that when he was lying at Craigweil House, near Bognor Regis, weak and exhausted after his long fight for life at the end of 1928, Lord Dawson of Penn (who died in 1945) and Sir Stanley Hewett, his two doctors in residence, advised that Princess Elizabeth, then nearly three, should be sent for to raise the King's languid spirits. Happy at her unexpected visit to the seaside, the little Princess played gaily with bucket and spade on the sand in front of her grandfather, while the doctors watched the effect of their new remedy for the depression of long convalescence. They had made a wise decision. The artless remarks of "Lilibet", as the Princess had by that time re-christened herself in her first attempts to pronounce her name, about what she was doing and what she intended to do, brought smiles to the invalid's cheeks, and it is a strange but vouched-for fact that a definite improvement in the King's general condition and spirits at once began to make itself evident. The doctor's remedy came not from the British Pharmacopoeia but from Lord Dawson's wide and deep knowledge of human nature—and it worked.

Between Princess Elizabeth and her mother and father no barriers of State or formality have ever existed. There were none in their Piccadilly home as Duke and Duchess of York, nor at Royal Lodge, the small country house which King George gave them near Windsor Castle: and none was permitted to develop after the accession.

King George VI, his consort, the Heiress to the Throne and her younger sister are, in their private lives, a normal, happily united, English family. The crown, sceptre and orb which, in the Coronation Service at Westminster, set the King apart from the people, have never been allowed to set him apart from his family. That has been Princess Elizabeth's supreme advantage. Heiress to the Throne, she has been able, to a greater extent than any of her predecessors, to enjoy the freedom of family life, to grow up a normal human being, with her personality entirely unspoilt by the fetters of State.

When Princess Elizabeth, daughter of Henry VIII, was a young woman of twenty in 1553, and her sister, Mary, came to the throne, she had to plead ignorance of the Catholic faith to excuse herself from attending Mass. Soon after, she was banished from her sister's Court, and later still, condemned to the Tower as a traitress. Till her sister's death and her own accession, her life was constantly in danger, her most innocent moves watched by Mary's spies, who did not scruple to twist them, whenever they could, into hints of treasonable activity.

Compare that tortuous life of suspicion with the free life of the Princess Elizabeth of our own day, and you have in essence the difference between the despotic autocracy of Tudor days and the leadership-by-example of the constitutional monarchy of Britain to-day.

Princesses, however enlightened and fond of their parents, cannot escape from all the penalties attaching to, and balancing the splendid advantages of, their exalted station. This was a lesson that Princess Elizabeth had to learn before she could talk, long before she had any conception that she was a princess.

It was less than nine months after her birth that the Duke and Duchess of York were compelled to say goodbye to their daughter, and leave her behind in the care of her two grandmothers, Queen Mary and the Countess of Strathmore (the Duchess's mother) while they set out in January 1927 on their six months' tour of Australia and New Zealand.

That first lesson in the duties of State passed unnoticed at the time over the fair-curled head of the baby Princess, who was happy enough spending the spring and summer days at Buckingham Palace, and at St. Paul's Walden, her other grandparents' home in Hertfordshire: it was the Duke and Duchess who felt the parting, able to watch their daughter's first developments only through the medium of photographs and lengthy nursery reports sent them by the two grandmothers and by the head nurse, Mrs. Knight. But not long afterwards, the Duchess would tell her baby about the journey "Mummy and Daddy" had made and describe the wonderful things they had seen, gradually explaining to her why it was that she had had to be left behind. While her parents were away, the little Princess learned to utter her first word: it was "Mummy", and when the Duke and Duchess reached Buckingham Palace after the ceremonial drive through London that marked the

Royal dolls, like others, must have their outings. Princess Elizabeth pushes her new bassinet.

QUEEN OF TO-MORROW

A picture that helped to make her "The Nation's Darling". The baby Princess wears her first jewellery, a coral necklace.

end of their long tour of Empire, Queen Mary had her granddaughter there to meet them, to use her carefully learned word for the first time to her real "Mummy" instead of to her photograph.

Queen Victoria let it be known in after life that, though there had been many happy moments in her youthful period of training and education at Kensington Palace, it was not a period to which she could ever look back with feelings of un-alloyed pleasure. One of her very earliest recollections, it is recorded, was of playing with the gold badge of the Garter belonging to Bishop Fisher of Salisbury, then Prelate of the Most Noble Order, and not much later she had to face what to our minds would be the intolerable ordeal of taking breakfast in the open with her mother, in full view of the strollers in Kensington Gardens.

Modern views on the natural rights of Royalty to have some of their privacy respected spared Princess Elizabeth that rather peculiar early introduction to the duty of appearing at ease in front of a crowd, and the days of her early training passed pleasantly and happily. But the railings round the gardens behind Hamilton Place, within the Park at Hyde Park Corner, became a regular afternoon rendezvous for Londoners who wanted to see Royalty at play in the years from 1928 onwards, for it was into these gardens, behind her home at 145, Piccadilly, that the Princess was taken daily, when the weather allowed, for exercise and play. Provincial relatives visiting London would be taken to the Gardens to stand for an hour or more for a glimpse of a white-shawled baby. Business men from the Dominions were charged by their wives to make it their duty to see the Princess on one of her outings, and would write home long and glowing (though perhaps not always entirely truthful) accounts of what they had seen through the railings. A little later, King George gave orders for one of the pair-horse landaus from the Royal Mews to be sent across to Piccadilly in the afternoon, to take the Princess for a drive round the Serpentine, a change in the Royal routine that drew bigger crowds than ever to see the baby. The Princess was a quick, observant child, and it did not take her long to grasp that the people she saw in the Park were anxious to see her. Obligingly, she would sit up on her nurse's knee, smiling and waving her little hand, to the delight of the crowds, and to the amusement of the straight-faced liveried Royal footmen sitting behind her.

Such precocious Royal gestures were definitely not encouraged, for it was the explicit wish of the Duke and Duchess that their daughter should be brought up unspoiled by

too early recognition of the position she undoubtedly enjoyed as the Empire's Baby. But it was obviously useless to attempt to disguise from her that the crowds *did* gather round to see her when she went out, while her friend and playmate from next-door, the daughter of Lord and Lady Allendale, could go out as often as she pleased, without attracting any crowds. Thus it was while she was still quite a baby that she learned she was a Princess; that though her father's house, with its tall, black, double doors and the brown-carpeted hall, where the two great ivory tusks of the elephant he had shot in Uganda stood on either side of the steps, was a private house, her grandfather's house, whose grey walls she could see from her nursery windows, was a Palace; and that her grandfather, whose bearded face was always smiling when he saw her, was a King and an Emperor. But if, as the Duchess read her fairy stories with their tales of Princesses who invariably "lived happily ever after", she remarked that she was a Princess herself, her mother would gently remind her that she was a real-life Princess, not one in a fairy-tale, and real-life Princesses, though they might make their lives happy, had lots of duties and tasks to perform which did not fall to their Royal sisters of fairyland.

In little ways like that, Princess Elizabeth was gradually accustomed to her future. Sometimes, as on her fourth birthday, which she spent at Windsor, she would be permitted to make a minor appearance in public. On that day, she solemnly "took the salute" from the Scots Guards, as they marched away after the changing of the Guard, with her elder boy cousins, the two sons of the Princess Royal (Viscount Lascelles and the Hon. Gerald Lascelles), whom she already knew were not Princes, though they, too, strangely enough, were the King's grandsons, standing a little behind her. The holiday crowds—it was Eastertide—cheered her, and running to the gates, she smiled at them, and waved delightedly.

Besides her mother and her grandmother, there was another woman, in a humbler sphere, who had a great influence on the development of Princess Elizabeth's character, to whom must justly be given some of the credit, too, for bringing both the Royal sisters up with an understanding of the value of manners, those outward symbols of an inward grace which William of Wykeham declared "makyeth man" and which assuredly may make, or mar, Princes and Princesses.

She was "Alla".

It was by this pet name that the Queen and both her daughters knew the late Mrs. Clara Cooper Knight, who, after growing old in the Queen's own service, spent some of the happiest years of her life as chief nurse to the Princesses. "Mrs." Knight—she had the title by the old-fashioned courtesy of "below-stairs", for she was never married—was the daughter of a yeoman farmer on the estates of the Queen's father, the Earl of Strathmore, at St. Paul's Walden, in Hertfordshire. As a girl of seventeen, she became under-nursery maid, helping to look after the then Lady

Out for a drive with "Alla": the Princesses and their nurse in 1931.

Beneath the grey walls of ancient Windsor Castle, the Queen watches her daughters at their lessons. The Princesses did their studies together in the open-air whenever possible.
Photograph: Studio Lisa.

Proud parenthood: the Duke and Duchess of York with their daughter.

Elizabeth Bowes-Lyon. It was Lady Elizabeth's baby attempts to pronounce her nurserymaid's name of Clara which resulted in "Alla", the designation which clung to her throughout the years. Between mistress and maid, a sincere and devoted attachment sprang up, an attachment which was to last right up to "Alla's" sudden death at Sandringham just after Christmas, 1945. The Queen and "Alla" understood each other perfectly, and the Queen knew that the upbringing of her daughters in all domestic matters could be in no better hands, nor could there be anyone else who would so exactly and intuitively carry out her own ideas and wishes, when State duties took her away from her children. One of the many things which Mrs. Knight knew very well was that the Queen wished her daughters to be brought up strictly and properly, with no laxity just because their father was King of England, but rather the reverse. So it was that "Alla", adoring slave of her young charges as she might be, always saw to it that they brushed and folded their clothes before going to bed as little girls, that they changed their shoes after a winter's day walk, in a word, that they took care of things and were not wasteful or neglectful.

That early training and the ingrained habits of tidiness it induced have never been forgotten by the Princesses, though to-day of course their clothes are looked after for them.

THE TRAINING OF A TWENTIETH-CENTURY PRINCESS

When Mrs. Knight died, the Queen and the two Princesses made the long journey from Sandringham in Norfolk to St. Paul's Walden in Hertfordshire to attend her funeral, a very marked expression of the regard in which they held this faithful woman who had given them a lifetime's devotion.

The Queen wrote on the card tied to her wreath of violets, "In loving and thankful memory from Elizabeth R." The Princesses, on their wreath of mixed flowers, tied a card inscribed, "In loving memory of Alla, from Elizabeth and Margaret."

As the time for more serious lessons approached, the future education of the Royal heiress of the third generation became a topic of paramount importance to be discussed at Royal family councils, and even to be considered by the Cabinet. It was, as has already been indicated, the firm conviction of the Duke and Duchess of York that their daughter should be brought up in as normal a manner as possible, but that she should not go to any of the fashionable girls' schools. There were several reasons operating to bring them to this decision. For one thing the choice of one school rather than another might have been regarded as invidious, and might well have provoked minor jealousies. For another, the selection of schoolmates for a girl who, even then, could easily be envisaged as the future Queen, might have made difficulties. Weightier still was the drawback that no ordinary girls' school curriculum would include all the subjects that it was felt one in the direct line of succession should study: nor would it be possible to give the desired and necessary emphasis to certain subjects of particular importance to the Princess without seriously disrupting the scheme of study for other girls at the school.

So, with the complete agreement of King George (necessary, since the reigning sovereign has a constitutional right to prescribe the education of members of the Royal family) and Queen Mary, and, with the approval of the Government of the day, who, traditionally, have a right to be informed of the educational progress of those in close proximity to the throne, it was decided that Princess Elizabeth should, for the time being, at any rate, be educated privately at home. This arrangement, which became a permanency, gave the added advantage of keeping the Princess within the family circle where, by example and precept, she could continue to absorb, as she had been doing up till then, the ways and manners of the Royal family. All that remained was to find a suitable person to be her instructress. Naturally, it was the Princess's mother who began to search for such a person, and her eyes at once turned to a young Scotswoman in the household of her sister, Lady Rose, who was married to Admiral Earl Granville (now Governor of Northern Ireland). This was Miss Marion Crawford, a twenty-five-year-old native of Dunfermline, who, after leaving Dunfermline High School, had gone on to take an honours degree at Edinburgh University. She had been governess first in the family of Lord Elgin, then had come to be governess to Lady Mary Leveson-Gower, the Duchess's niece. Lady Granville recommended her daughter's governess very highly, and in 1933, when the Princess was seven years old, Miss Crawford came to the Duchess to start her daughter on the highroad of learning. She remained with Princess Elizabeth until a few weeks before her Royal charge's wedding, when she herself married, to return to Buckingham Palace as Mrs. George Buthlay, to continue duty as governess to Princess Margaret.

"Crawfie" as she quickly came to be known in the Royal family circle, was an ideal choice. Quiet, reserved in manner, with a wide and far-ranging intelligence, she combined the qualities of firmness—very necessary in the case of a highly self-confident

Princess—with an affectionate charm that won her Royal pupil's heart from the beginning. After the Princess became a grown young woman, "Crawfie" remained one of her closest intimates, one of her most trusted confidantes and advisers; but no one outside the Royal circle ever heard "Crawfie" talk about her Royal charge. She was always content to remain in the background, shrinking from any form of publicity, and yet forming a most valuable link between the Princess and the outer world.

Keen on foreign travel, she would spend her holidays abroad, where no one meeting the self-contained, brown-haired Scotswoman who seemed to know so much of local history, would dream that she had charge of the education of the future Queen of England. When she came home, the Princess would hear from her of life in other countries, gaining a vicarious, but valuable, insight into the ways of other lands. Baroness Lehzen, who filled a like office to Queen Victoria, used to address her Royal pupil as "Madam", and treated her, to judge from contemporary accounts, in a manner that, to modern taste, seems a little priggish. No such charge could be brought against Miss Crawford. Between her and her two pupils—for Princess Margaret, a few years later, came to join her sister's studies—there always existed a most happy and natural relationship unstrained in any way.

On public occasions, she would address the Princess with the "Ma'am" of formality, but in the classroom, it was simply "Princess", or in earlier days, more simply still "Elizabeth". Princess Elizabeth, and the Empire at large, owe a great debt to this Scotswoman of sterling character and uprightness, who has taught her much besides mere book reading, and no assessment of the Princess could be complete without tribute to the good influence of Miss Crawford.

History, geography, arithmetic, algebra, English grammar and literature were among the Princess's early studies, and of these, history was easily a first favourite, enlivened often by stories not to be found in the history books, stories of family connections and ancestors who had played their part and left their mark on the European scene. Shakespeare, too, was made more vivid for the Princess when she came to read Macbeth, and could so easily conjure up the worn steps of the circular stone staircase, the deep embrasured windows of Glamis Castle, her summer holiday home, as a background for the sonorous periods of the great drama: or realise, when she read Henry V, that it was of her own ancestor-King that Shakespeare wrote. All these aids to Royal learning, which fitted so easily and well into the scheme of education at home, would have been a hundred times more difficult at school.

But though her lessons were done in the friendly atmosphere of her own home, in the familiar surroundings of an upstairs room at Piccadilly, set aside for exclusive use as a schoolroom, the Princess was not allowed any more laxity—indeed, rather less—than girls at school. School hours were regularly set, and regularly adhered to, and, by an early and a wise decision of the Duke and Duchess of York, were regarded as having first and overriding call on the Royal pupil's time. It is easy to imagine what confusion the Princess's schoolwork could easily have fallen into had this rule not been applied, and had, instead, public outings and functions been allowed to interfere with the programme of lessons. That was emphatically not the way the Duke and Duchess wanted their daughter to be trained, and Miss Crawford saw to it that pressure from any and every quarter to break into the educational routine was stoutly and strongly resisted.

THE TRAINING OF A TWENTIETH-CENTURY PRINCESS

With a naturally quick brain and a lively intelligence, the Princess profited to the full under this system of disciplined, though not forced, education. She showed an early aptitude for English, a liking for, and skill in, composition, that remain with her to-day so that, if, at any time in the future, any of her writings are made public—not that there is much likelihood of this happening—her prose style would show her a worthy descendant of Queen Victoria, to whose clarity of thought and vigour of expression (if slightly marred by a predilection for italics and underlinings) her published letters are sufficient testimony. She was, in the main, a diligent pupil, slightly impatient to advance at a faster pace than was always considered wise, but with a memory so retentive, and a mental grasp so eager, of any subject in which she was really interested, that the greater speed was many times justified.

To the Duchess, who had been taught French in her early infancy—a happy circumstance that enables the Queen of England to-day to talk with ease, fluency and an almost faultless accent to the citizens of France in their own language—it seemed that the earlier her daughter began to learn a second language, the better. Princess Elizabeth began to lisp French words nearly as soon as she started to speak English, learning them at her mother's knee, an early foundation which caused her first native French instructress

*The Princesses explore the wonders of the "smallest port in the world":
at the model village of "Bekonscot", Bucks.*

An early occasion of State: the Princesses drive with their parents to the Silver Jubilee Service of their grandfather.

to wonder at the purity of her accent. "French only" periods, including meal-times, were the frequent rule in the Royal nursery. During these, anything said in any other language was ignored, a practice which continued until quite recent days. The Princess still has, as one of her close friends and personal companions, a Belgian lady, Madame la Comtesse de Bellaigue, who became attached to the Royal household as senior French tutor and companion to the Princess during the war.

To-day, French is a natural second language to the Princess. She can read, write and express herself as clearly in French as in her native English, and has a wider and deeper acquaintance with French literature and verse than many Frenchmen. She is familiar with the works of the great classic masters, Molière, Racine, Corneille, to name but a few, and with the writings of modern French authors as well. She can quote long passages from Du Bellay, Malherbe, Lamartine and Hugo, as well as many of the sonnets and rondels of Villon and Ronsard. When she broadcast to the children of newly-liberated Belgium early in 1945, so perfect was her delivery, so pure and free from English accent her enunciation, that a famous actor of the Comédie Française, who had coached novice speakers on the BBC's European transmissions during the war, said to me as he listened,

THE TRAINING OF A TWENTIETH-CENTURY PRINCESS

"Elle fait à merveille: on croit vraiment c'est une Française qui parle." Tears rolled down that famous French actor's cheeks as he listened to the simple words of the eighteen-year-old British Princess expressing her country's thanks to the children of Belgium for their Christmas gift of toys to the boys and girls of Britain. When the Princess paid her first visit to France at Whitsun 1948, she was surprised and delighted at the number of men and women who yielded their hearts to her at the memory of that one short radio talk.

That French should come easily to the Princess is not surprising. Not only her mother, but also her aunt, the Princess Royal, spoke the language so well as a girl that at the early age of twelve she drew from the French Ambassador of the day congratulations on her "charming and fluent" pronunciation of his language.

French was not the only language Princess Elizabeth learned in her schoolroom. When war began, she was already well advanced with her German studies, and a hard decision had to be reached. Should these studies be discontinued, on the narrow precedent of the 1914–18 war, because we were again at war, this time with Nazi Germany, or should the Princess continue normally in the course set for her? In spite of the risk of ill-founded criticism, which, happily, was not forthcoming, the King decided that the language of

Another State drive: this time to see their father and mother crowned King and Queen.

39

At the Coronation Service: Princess Elizabeth studies the Order of Service, while Queen Mary explains a late Queen Maud of Norway is on Queen Mary's

Schiller and Goethe was much greater and more lasting than the ephemeral Third Reich of Herr Hitler, and he could see no need to deprive his daughter of a knowledge of the great storehouse of German literature merely because the present-day users of that language were attempting to destroy the rest of civilisation. So the Princess continued to study German, though not, perhaps, with quite the same enthusiasm as she displayed for French.

The Princess was never allowed to imagine that there is any easy Royal road to learning even for those of Royal birth. She had to devote as much care and time to her three favourite subjects, English, history and French, as to others, like arithmetic and algebra, which she absorbed more slowly and with less zest. In the days when she sat alone in her classroom at Piccadilly, or later, when she sat with Princess Margaret in the schoolroom at Buckingham Palace where her father and uncles had done their early studies, the Royal pupil, just like any other girl, had to plough through the rules of grammar, to conjugate

r. Both Princesses wear their coronets. Next to Princess Margaret is her aunt, the Princess Royal. The
the Duchesses of Gloucester and Kent next to her.

verbs, regular and irregular, to parse and analyse sentences, to memorise place names and
battle dates. In her case, thoroughness of grounding was even more rigidly insisted on—
and much more easy to enforce—than with a group of girls studying together. That does
not mean that all lessons were made dull. On the contrary, Miss Crawford kept it as a
guiding principle to make them all as interesting and stimulating as possible, and all
sorts of outside aids were brought in to this end. Geography, for instance, which was not
among the Princess's early favourites, was made more attractive by tales of the overseas
visits of members of her family, and of course, the family motif ran through many of the
early English history lessons. At Buckingham Palace there were many souvenirs of overseas visits and gifts from foreign visitors which served as starting points for interest in one
country or another. This was particularly so, naturally, in the case of the Dominions and
India, and the British colonies.

A rug which the Princess used for many years whenever she went out for a motor ride illustrates this aspect of the carefully planned training devised for her. The rug, of warm shaggy sheepskin, backed by thick blue cloth, looked ordinary enough, comfortably tucked round the Princess and whoever might be her companion in the car. The secret was on the back. Outlined in bold yellow stitching against the blue ground was an exact and accurate map of Australia, showing the divisions of the States and Territories, each with its name or initials. No one, using that mapped rug for any length of time, could help but have the contours of the Commonwealth engraved, almost unconsciously, on their mind.

Based on much the same educational principles, visits to the Tower of London, the museums of South Kensington, and other places of historical importance form a usual part of present day school-training. Princess Elizabeth and Princess Margaret had the advantage, when they made their round of such visits in the spring and early summer of 1939, while the King and Queen were away on their tour of Canada and their visit to the United States, of having their grandmother, Queen Mary, as their mentor and guide. Probably no one outside the regular staffs of the various museums has anything like such a deep and detailed knowledge of the historical exhibits, particularly those with Royal associations, in our great national collections, as has Queen Mary. She gladly consented to take her grandchildren on a "grand tour" of the London treasure houses, and enthusiastic accounts of all they had seen with her went from the Princesses across the Atlantic to the King and Queen. After hearing her tell them legends and stories of the past made vivid for them by what they saw, the Monument, Traitors' Gate at the Tower,

A drive in the Highlands with her parents and her grandfather, King George V. Princess Elizabeth has always loved Balmoral, the Royal home on Deeside.

the Elgin Marbles at the British Museum, and so on, the Royal sisters would go back to the drier side of their historical studies with renewed and invigorated zeal.

In the midst of all this serious preparation for the earnest life to come, the Princess remained a happy, unspoilt little girl, so natural and free from self-importance that even the great excitement of the coronation did not turn her head.

A couple of months after those never-to-be-forgotten festivities, Princess Elizabeth found herself one evening with Princess Margaret in their sleeping saloon on the Royal train, drawn up at the Euston platform awaiting the arrival of the King and Queen on their way north to Balmoral. The Princesses had been brought to the station

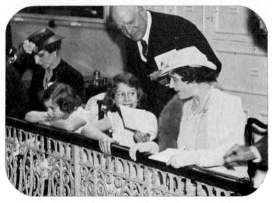

"Mama" explains: the Princess had the same smile when a young girl as she has today. They and Princess Margaret are watching the children's swimming competition at the Bath Club.

early to be put to bed on the train at their usual time. A railway policeman, pacing the platform, after the Royal nurses had made their way to their own part of the train, was surprised to hear a tapping, regular and distinct, coming from the windows of the Royal train. Doubtless with some thoughts of madmen and train wreckers in mind, he approached the window more closely, to see the blind drawn back, and Princess Elizabeth trying to attract his attention. "Please, policeman, go and get us a comic paper to read," pleaded the heiress of England, holding out a shilling in her hand through the opened window. "Please!" There was nothing in his instructions telling him what to do in a case like this, so the slightly bewildered constable, not used to receiving direct Royal requests, walked off to the bookstall, purchased the "comics", and handed them through the window with the change to the very grateful eleven-year-old inside.

But he did not pay for the papers with the Princess's shilling. He used another coin of his own for that, keeping the Royal shilling as a treasured souvenir.

Formal examinations, the Junior Oxford Locals, which her mother had passed as a young girl, and later, the Senior Schools, and Matriculation, were not, it was laid down, to come the Princess's way, since her studies were based on a more specialised plan, but the indispensable check that graded examinations at regular intervals give on school progress was obtained simply by the setting of papers designed especially for the Princess, yet based on the general average standard of her age. Consistently, she gained excellent marks, assessing her as definitely of above average intelligence, and these results were made the more reliable by the fact that steps were taken to see that the examiners did not always know whose papers they were marking.

The overall master plan for the Princess's education laid down in her earliest years by her father and mother, in agreement with King George V and Queen Mary, needed very little alteration, but soon the time came when more specialised and advanced studies called for extra tuition in addition to that of Miss Crawford. The claims of many eminent and leading figures in the scholastic world were given most careful review before this important choice was made. Finally, the King gave approval to the appointment as chief tutor to the Princess of one of the most highly regarded of living historians, Mr. (now Sir) Clarence Henry Kennett Marten, at that time Vice-Provost, now Provost, of Eton College, renowned alike for his profound knowledge of history both classical and modern, and for his individual and highly successful approach to the teaching of it.

That decision has never been regretted either by the King and Queen, by Sir Henry Marten, or by Princess Elizabeth. Seldom can a happier choice have been made. History, world history, British, European, American, political and economic history, is necessarily the subject of primary importance in the education of those to whose lot it must fall to take some part, greater or smaller, in the making of the history of the future. A sound basis of knowledge of the mistakes, as well as the successes of the past, is an essential to good judgement on the problems of the present, and it was the high task of the new tutor to see that the Princess was guided along the ways of learning in such fashion as to give her this qualification for wise decision on the multifarious problems that one day will be brought to her. The outward mark and sign of the success with which he has acquitted himself of that charge is to be found in the signal honour which the King did him when, on Sunday, March 4, 1945, he knighted him and invested him with the insignia of a Knight Commander of the Royal Victorian Order—the personal order of the Royal Family, bestowed only for direct and personal service to members of it, without recommendation from political quarters—on the steps of Eton College Chapel, in the open air, in full view of the Eton boys.

The deeper and more significant sign of his success lies in the finely trained brain with its deep background of accurate, well-digested knowledge, that is Princess Elizabeth's to-day.

Sir Henry, known to all Etonians as "Shee-Kay" from his own pronunciation of his initials, has been sixty years at Eton. He was educated at Eton and then at Balliol College, Oxford, where he took a First Class in Modern History. He returned to Eton in 1896 at the age of twenty-four, as an assistant master of brilliant young promise. He became successively a house master, Lower Master, from 1925-29, Vice Provost in 1929, and finally Provost in 1945. President of the Historical Association from 1929-31, he has written much about history and its teaching, and has played a major part in bringing about the modern attitude to history as a study of the vast, complex changes in, and the evolution of, human society, rather than an absorption in national movements and the duration of dynasties and the lives of Kings.

Some slight idea of the depth and variety of the Princess's studies may be gauged from the fact that such unusual, but vastly important, subjects as the history of British agriculture, and the theory and law of land tenure, were included among the special subjects which she studied under Sir Henry.

When Prince Albert Edward, afterwards King Edward VII, was eighteen, in 1859, his father, the Prince Consort, called a conference of educational leaders at Edinburgh, in May, to review the question of the future education of the heir to the throne. As a result, it was decided that the Prince should spend a time at both Oxford and Cambridge—thus avoiding any hurt to the feelings of either University—with a programme of study which the late Sir George Arthur described as a "colossal curriculum, with the addition of indigestible learning." Prince Albert Edward in after life became famous for "knowing everything that is not in books, and little that is," perhaps as a revolt from this early attempt to cram too much bookish lore into his young mind.

That danger did not confront Princess Elizabeth. Though, as has been indicated, her studies and curriculum were at various stages the subject of family talks within the Royal circle, and though the Cabinet took a constant, if not a very close or detailed, interest in her educational progress, the mistake of putting the question of her future training to semi-public debate at a formal educational conference was never made, nor was there any attempt at forcing too much learning on her too quickly.

Yet the Princess, who was eighteen in 1944, had problems to study which were certainly not the concern of her great-grandfather ninety-five years beforehand. American history, for example, was a closed book to Albert Edward when he went to the United States in 1859-60, and the history of the Dominion of Canada had yet to be written when he journeyed through it on that same tour *incognito* as "Lord Renfrew", for the British North America Act, under which the Dominion came into being, was still seven years distant in the future. And before Princess Elizabeth came of full age the implications of the atom bomb, the rivalry between Communism and free democracy, the uncertain future of the United Nations Organisation had added themselves to the world problems confronting her.

Princess Elizabeth had studied the history of each of the four great Dominions, as well as Indian history: and the economic and political development of each, as well. She has read—as too few of her father's subjects have read—Muzzey's *History of the United States*, and many other books and papers on the history of the Republic besides that great standard work. She is probably better acquainted with the history and development of the United States than a good many American girls of her age, and she is certainly the very first heir to the British throne to be brought up with a full understanding and realisation of the growth and rise to power of our great sister democracy. Even as late as the King's own young days, the teaching of American history was apt to stop short at a sketchy, and not always accurate, account of the War of Independence of 1775–82, and the Civil War of 1860–65. Princess Elizabeth's teaching and reading went far beyond the Boston Tea Party and the march of Stonewall Jackson, deep into the causes underlying the two struggles, the effects of the outcome of each, and the general progress of the American people after them. Nor was she taught to read history through rose-coloured

The Princess calms her cousin: at the christening of Prince Richard of Gloucester, his brother, Prince William, was shy.

The smile that wins all hearts: Princess Elizabeth, President of the Queen Elizabeth Hospital for Children, Hackney, cheers a small patient.

glasses. The Boer war, its causes and effects, the French problem in Canada, and other Dominion difficulties past and present have been put before her without disguise.

Economics, economic history, and British constitutional history, are all subjects in which the Princess is well versed. Her reading has been wide and catholic, ranging in English from Shakespeare's plays, Chaucer's *Canterbury Tales*, the poems of Keats, Coleridge, Browning and Tennyson, to Dickens, Scott, Trollope, Stevenson, Conan Doyle and John Buchan, in French from Daudet's *Lettres de Mon Moulin* to Foncin's *Geographie Historique*.

Nowadays, as a married woman, the Princess still continues a certain amount of reading of a post-graduate nature in some of the subjects, history prime among them, which have always been her special interests.

The fact that she was never subject to any "cramming" can best be seen from her school timetable as a girl. Lessons began at 9.30 precisely, after schoolroom breakfast which she took alone with her governess. At eleven o'clock, there was a "break" for walking or riding—mostly in Windsor Great Park—with lessons resumed again at 11.45.

In the afternoon, the programme varied with the season and the weather. At least two hours of work were expected of the Royal pupil, but often these would be devoted to subjects of a lighter nature, drawing, or, in summer, sketching out of doors. That was the regime under Miss Crawford and her women teachers for French and German. Later, when her studies under Sir Henry Marten became more serious and intensified, the hours were prolonged, the afternoons devoted more to serious reading—though much of this was done in the open air—and a good deal of the evenings spent in written preparation.

Never interfering with those to whom she had entrusted her daughter's education, but always watchful in the background, the Queen supervised every detail of the education of Princess Elizabeth, and still acts in the same way to Princess Margaret whose training is following much the same course as that of her sister.

One other, and most important, aspect of the training of the Princess concerns religion. Quite apart from the fact that when she comes to Queenship the Princess will occupy a special position, carry special responsibilities, as head of the Established Church, she has been brought up by her parents in the simple, Christian faith that is theirs. Scriptural history and studies, under the guidance of Canon Crawley, of St. George's Chapel, Windsor, took a prominent place in her early studies. In matters of religion, it is the home and family influence that are most important, and in no home in the Empire is there a couple of more sincere and devout religious persuasion than the King and Queen. Regular attendance at church is, and has always been, a dominant feature in the life of the Royal family circle, and it is a rare thing indeed for Princess Elizabeth to miss morning service, no matter where she may be.

She was christened on May 29, 1926, in the private chapel of Buckingham Palace, the chapel which, fifteen years later, was to be shattered by a German bomb.

Traditional observance and high ceremony properly surrounded this occasion of great import. The fair-haired baby girl who one day might occupy her grandfather's position as the temporal head of the Church of England, was baptised by the Archbishop of York (the late Lord Lang of Lambeth), assisted by Prebendary Percival, Precentor of the Chapels Royal and Domestic Chaplain to the King.

QUEEN OF TO-MORROW

Her four grandparents, the King and Queen and the Earl and Countess of Strathmore, her parents, the Duke and Duchess of York, her uncles and aunt, the Prince of Wales, Prince Henry and Princess Mary, and a number of other close relatives, were the only witnesses of the ceremony, at which the choir of the Chapel Royal sang. She had six sponsors, King George and Queen Mary, Princess Mary, the veteran Duke of Connaught, last surviving son of Queen Victoria, the Earl of Strathmore, and her maternal aunt, Lady Elphinstone.

Her christening robe of old ivory lace was itself an heirloom of Royalty, for it had been worn by four future sovereigns of England in turn at their christenings, Queen Victoria, King Edward VII, King George V, and King Edward VIII, as well as by the Empress Frederick, Queen Victoria's daughter. Water for the Royal baptism had been brought from the River Jordan, as was the custom at all Royal christenings, and the "Lily Font", a gold bowl used at the christenings of all Queen Victoria's descendants born in this country, was brought to the Palace from Windsor Castle for the occasion.

Sixteen years later, after receiving a special course of instruction from her early religious mentor, Canon Crawley, the Princess was confirmed, in the tiny circular private chapel at Windsor Castle. Dr. Lang, now Archbishop of Canterbury, assisted by the Dean of Windsor, Dr. Baillie, administered the rite on March 28, 1942. Afterwards, the Archbishop preached a short sermon, in which he reminded the young Princess of the high and dread responsibilities of the station to which it had pleased God to call her. Princess Elizabeth took her first communion privately on the following Sunday.

The armorial bearings of H.R.H. The Princess Elizabeth and H.R.H. the Duke of Edinburgh. These photographs were taken by special permission from the original parchment warrants of the grant-of-arms at the College of Arms.

Photograph: Fox Photos Ltd.

The Coats of Arms

Princess Elizabeth was granted her coat-of-arms by the King on her eighteenth birthday. Since she is a Princess of the Blood Royal, her arms were not changed by her marriage, though the Garter given her by her father on her wedding eve now appears surrounding the "lozenge" which in Royal Arms replaces the shield. Her arms are the Royal Arms of England, "differenced", in the heraldic terms with a "cadency label of devices" indicating her position as a "cadet" of the House of Windsor.

The label is of three points argent, on the centre point charged with the Tudor Rose, the two others with the Cross of St. George. The King personally chose these devices, in accordance with the ancient rules of coat-armour, unchanged since the days of Crecy, when visored knights had no means of identifying friend or foe save by their blazoned shields. The white rose of York, not previously used for such a purpose, was chosen by the King in allusion to the fact that, before his accession, he was Duke, and his daughter Princess, of York. Both the lion and unicorn supporters, as well as the lozenge, are charged with the label.

Though the days when Princes and Princesses displayed their coat-armour have gone by, the Princess's arms still to-day serve as a means of identifying her, for the Royal Arms with her cadency label form her personal standard or, more correctly, banner, which she is entitled to fly over her own house or, as a Royal person, over any house where she may be dwelling, save when a senior ranking member of her family—the King or Queen or Queen Mary—is in residence at the same time. It is this banner which, flying from the radiator of her car, gives a clear indication to waiting crowds where to look for the Princess.

Arms of the Duke of Edinburgh, with his shield also encircled by the Garter, are more complex than those of his wife. They show, heraldically, the Duke's descent from the three Royal Houses of Great Britain, Greece and Denmark, and include the devices of sixteen different countries. The full blazon is:

Arms: The Royal Arms of Greece, charged in the dexter chief point with an escutcheon of the arms of Princess Alice, his mother, namely the Royal Arms of Britain differenced by a label of three points argent, on the centre point charged with a rose gules, and each of the other points with an ermine spot sable. The Royal Arms of Greece are azure, a Greek cross argent, surmounted by an inescutcheon of four principal quarters, quarterly first, or, semée of hearts gules, three lions passant in pale azure, ducally crowned or (for Denmark): second, or, two lions passant in pale azure (for Sondergylland-Slesvig): third, per fesse the chief azure, three crowns or (for Scandinavia) the base composed of three coats, namely, on the dexter side gules a stock-fish (or dried cod) argent crowned or (for Iceland), on the sinister side, in chief azure a ram statant argent (for the Faroe Islands), and in base azure, a bear sejant errect argent (for Greenland): and, fourth, per fesse, in chief or, a lion passant in chief azure, the base semée of hearts gules (for Gothland), and in base gules a wyvern passant and crowned or (for Vandalia): over the four grand quarters an escutcheon of four coats, namely one, gules an inescutcheon per fesse argent, and of the field, between three passion nails in pairle points towards the centre, and as many demi-nettle-leaves, also argent (for Holstein): two, gules, a swan with wings elevated argent, ducally gorged gules (for Stormarn): three, gules, a cavalier on horseback, holding in his dexter hand a sword (for Ditmarsken): four, gules, a horse's head couped or (for Lauenborg): and over all an inescutcheon of the family arms of the Counts of Oldenborg: namely or, two bars gules (for Oldenborg): impaling azure a crosse-patée alesée or (for Delmenhorst).

Crest: A plume of five Ostrich feathers, alternately sable and argent issuant from a Ducal Coronet or (these feathers are derived from the Carisbrooke and Mountbatten arms).

Supporters: Dexter, a representation of Heracles, girt about the loins with a lion skin, crowned with a chaplet of oak leaves, and holding in the dexter hand a Club proper. Sinister, a lion queue forchée, ducally crowned or, and gorged with a naval coronet azure.

Coronet: A coronet composed of crosses-patées and fleur-de-lys alternately or. This coronet is similar to that on the Princess's arms, and is generally used to denote the younger sons of Kings. The helmet, full-face (or affrontée) is also a sign of Royal rank.

The colour photographs of the arms of the Princess and the Duke are of the actual parchment warrants bearing the original grants of arms. They were taken by special permission at the College of Arms.

The Princesses wear their coronets: with the new-crowned King and Queen and Queen Mary on the balcony of Buckingham Palace, Coronation Day, May 12, 1937.

CHAPTER THREE

Her Place in the Constitution

MARRIAGE has not affected the place of Princess Elizabeth in the line of succession, nor has it altered her constitutional position. She is, and will remain throughout the lifetime of her father, Heiress Presumptive to the Throne. Her husband, the Duke of Edinburgh, has no place in the line of succession. If and when Princess Elizabeth succeeds to the Throne, he will be Prince Consort—if Parliament and the Queen decide to invest him with that non-hereditary title—without any greater constitutional position or power than is to-day enjoyed by Her Majesty the Queen as Consort of the Sovereign.

What must materially affect the line of succession is the birth of a baby, boy or girl, to the Princess and the Duke. Their child, of whichever sex, automatically displaces Princess Margaret from her present position as second in succession, because the Crown descends in the direct line, male or female. The same rules govern the children of Princess Elizabeth as governed her own position as elder daughter of the King. A son born to her takes precedence over any of his sisters, no matter how much older they might be. Her daughters must rank for succession in order of birth, immediately followed by Princess Margaret.

The last occasion on which the question of the succession to the Throne became an immediate question was on the night of August 21, 1930.

That evening, a heavy thunderstorm broke over the little town of Forfar, in the county of Angus, Scotland. Lightning flashed across the greying summer sky, rolls of thunder reverberated across the vale of Strathmore, echoed back from the forest-clad hills. Within the massive stone walls of Glamis Castle, the ancient home of Macbeth, whose name Shakespeare wove for ever into the pattern of British history, the thunder seemed to those waiting to provide a sombre accompaniment to the great event that was at last taking place after many long days of dragging expectancy.

Through the pelting rain, a fast driven car came to the tall iron gates, blazoned with the arms of the Earls of Strathmore, its headlights throwing into sudden prominence the strange "Beasts of Glamis" whose stone-carved effigies figure the outer walls of the Castle grounds. Police, their flat caps, with blue and white diced bands of Scotland, and their oilskin capes dripping with water, saluted as the car passed. In it was the stocky figure of Mr. J. R. Clynes, the former cotton worker who was then His Majesty's Principal Secretary of State for Home Affairs. He had just been summoned by telephone to Glamis Castle from "the Bonnie Hoose o' Airlie"—otherwise Airlie Castle, half a dozen miles away, near Kirriemuir—where he was staying with the Dowager Countess of Airlie. The little crowd of villagers and pressmen waiting outside the Castle gates knew, when they saw him drive in, that the hour they had been so long awaiting had arrived, for the mission that had brought Mr. Clynes some five hundred miles from

TELEPHONE NO. 4.

GLAMIS CASTLE,
GLAMIS,
N.B.

Her Royal Highness The Duchess of York gave birth to a daughter this evening

Both Her Royal Highness & The Infant Princess are making very satisfactory progress

*Henry Simson F.C.O.G. F.R.C.S.Edin.
F.R.C.P*

+ Neon Reynolds F.R.C.S.Edin.

*David Myles M.B.Ch.B.
Glamis*

A document of history: the bulletin announcing the birth of Princess Margaret, photographed from the original.

HER PLACE IN THE CONSTITUTION

Whitehall to one remote Scottish castle, where for two weeks he had been transacting the business of the Home Office under some difficulties, and that now sent him hurrying through the storm to another, was to carry out his constitutional duty of testifying to the birth of a new grandchild to King George V, who, boy or girl, would be in direct line of succession to the Throne.

Until fairly recent times, this duty, which dates back to the days when Royal changelings might be foisted on the people, had been carried out to the letter by successive Home Secretaries, who were compelled to be present at the actual birth or at least, in an adjoining room. But this distasteful task had been lightened at the suggestion of the Prince Consort, when the future Edward VII was born at Buckingham Palace in 1841, and the immediate personal presence of the Home Secretary has not been deemed necessary since then, though he must be within close call, and his department remains, to this day, the official channel through which all Royal births are announced.

Mr. Clynes was not surprised therefore when the Duke of York met him at the great door of Glamis with the news that the baby was already born. But he was eager, as the whole nation and empire were eager, to know if it was a Prince or a Princess that he was about to see. The Duke told him it was a daughter.

That one word meant all the difference to the future of Princess Elizabeth. Had the Duchess's second child been a son, Princess Elizabeth of York would have been no longer third, but fourth, in succession to the crown her grandfather still wore, and this would have changed, drastically changed, her life from then on. With a sister, and not a brother, added to her family, she remained the first of the new generation in the line of succession, and, in a sense, her training for the responsibilities of future Queenship began to take more definite shape from that moment.

The three doctors attending the Duchess, Dr. David Myles, a St. Andrews man, who was the local physician, the late Sir Henry Simson, the gynaecologist, and Mr. F. Neon Reynolds, the surgeon and anaesthetist, sat down to write their bulletin, while the Duke sent off telegrams to the King and Queen, aboard the Royal yacht at Cowes, and to other members of the Royal family, and Mr. Clynes completed his constitutional duty by despatching a telegram conveying the news to the Lord Mayor of London.

Meanwhile, the growing crowd at the Castle gates were becoming impatient. They still knew nothing, and it was a full hour later before the doctors' bulletin was read out in the little village street of Glamis, to be flashed by telephone to the waiting newspaper offices in London, standing by with their presses held. For the long period of waiting, the importance attaching to the sex of the new baby, the romantic setting for the birth, had all combined to bring public interest to excitement point.

There was a certain feeling of regret at the absence of a new male in the direct line of succession: but there was general satisfaction that the four-years-old Princess, who had already won herself a place as the nation's darling, was not to be displaced by a baby Prince.

After the high-spirited celebrations in Glamis village and the neighbourhood had died down, after the bonfires lit to mark the birth of the first Royal Princess to be born in Scotland for 300 years had burned out, students of genealogy began to busy themselves with the question of whether the arrival of the new Princess of York did not, in fact, alter the position of her elder sister in relation to the succession. Basing their arguments on the legal position that the law of primogeniture applies in this country only to male heirs of private estates, they put forward the theory that the two Royal sisters shared equal rights, just as is the case with two daughters of a peer or other landowner, however great the difference in their ages. In such a case, the title, according to the ancient law of succession, goes into abeyance, and the property is shared equally.

To-day, when Princess Elizabeth is universally recognised as the sole heiress to the Throne, the question may seem remote and academic, but at the time, and, indeed, throughout the next ten years, it was raised repeatedly in various quarters, without any really authoritative pronouncement being made. Genealogists, laboriously searching the records, found that the problem of which of two Royal sisters should succeed had arisen in the past, to be settled by specific Acts of Parliament, as in the case of Princess Mary and Princess Elizabeth, the daughters of Henry VIII, and in the case of the two daughters of James II, Mary and Anne, whose succession to the crown in that order was determined under the Bill of Rights. Hence, they concluded, the succession to the Throne had always followed the same rules as applied to real property until the reforms made under Lord Birkenhead as Lord Chancellor, which meant that the two Princesses would inherit equally as co-heiresses. Constitutional lawyers, realising that such a position would be intolerable, urged the necessity for passing legislation to settle the order of succession and to establish the constitutional position of the elder Princess. By one of those fascinating twists of legal precedent, the question of equal inheritance did not, it was stressed, arise in the case of the Crown of Scotland because the interpretation of the Scots peerage law allowed an elder daughter to succeed in preference to her younger sister. This, again, could be challenged on the legitimate score that the Act of Union, passed in 1706, included provision for the terms of the Act of Settlement of 1700 (which ruled that the Crown, and "all honours, styles, titles, regalities, prerogatives, powers, jurisdictions and authorities" should descend through Princess Sophia, Electress of Hanover and granddaughter of James I, to "the heirs of her body being Protestants") to apply equally to Scotland, thenceforth united with England in the Kingdom of Great Britain.

In the next editions of Debrett, and Burke's Peerage (for 1931), the position of the new Princess of the House of Windsor, H.R.H. Margaret Rose of York, was mentioned. It was stated by Burke that "As a result of an inquiry into the constitutional position, the Royal Princess has been declared fourth in succession to the Throne", while Debrett made the point in a similar way. But this did not satisfy the constitutional purists. Law Officers of the Crown had studied the question very closely, on the orders of King George V, and had reported privately that the right of Princess Elizabeth to succeed before her younger sister was unimpeachable and needed no special Act of Parliament to confirm it. But their findings had neither been reported by the Prime Minister of the day, nor otherwise made public.

When the Duke of York succeeded as King George VI, the matter became of much greater urgency, as the Princess was now the immediate heiress to the Throne. Two months after the accession, the question was finally cleared up through the medium of question-and-answer in the House of Commons.

On January 28, 1937, Mr. Geoffrey Mander, Liberal M.P. for Wolverhampton (East), asked the Home Secretary (Sir John, now Viscount, Simon) whether it was proposed to introduce legislation to amend the Act of Settlement with a view to making clear that the Princess Elizabeth was the sole heir to the Throne, and did not share it jointly with her sister on the analogy of the Peerage Law. Sir John's reply was a declaration of first-rate constitutional importance, for it settled the question of succession without room for further quibbling. He said: "No, sir: there is no reason to do so. His Majesty's Government are advised that there is no doubt that in the present circumstances Her Royal Highness the Princess Elizabeth would succeed to the Throne as sole heir."

From then on, no one has been able to question the undoubted position of the King's elder daughter as his heiress presumptive: nor could any similar doubts arise if Princess Elizabeth should have two or more daughters. Yet, in the minds of the general public, as distinct from those who make a study of the constitution, there still seems to remain room for doubt of another kind, doubt, in this case, as to the exact implication of the phrase "Heiress Presumptive". This doubt can be quickly and easily cleared up. Had a son been born to Their Majesties at any time since the accession, he would have been, at birth, Duke of Cornwall, and *Heir Apparent* to the Throne, thus displacing his elder sister as next in succession to her father, and making Princess Margaret third instead of second, in the line. That is a hypothetical, or presumptive case, and it is precisely on the presumption that there will be no male child of a Sovereign that his daughter remains his heir, unless and until a son is born. Princess Elizabeth can therefore never become Heiress Apparent, for as long as her father lives, the legal and constitutional presumption that he might have a son must be maintained.

It is for the same reason, namely that the law must always take into account the possibility of the birth of further children during the father's lifetime, that the Dukedom of Cornwall, together with the rich estates that appertain to it, cannot be bestowed by the King on Princess Elizabeth. They must remain in abeyance for the use of any future first-born son of the Sovereign.

If no son is born to his present Majesty, the Royal Dukedom will remain vested in the Crown until such time as there is a son born to the reigning Sovereign of the day. A son born to Princess Elizabeth could not be Duke of Cornwall until his mother had succeeded as queen.

This question of a new title became a matter of public interest as the Princess's eighteenth birthday approached. For Royalty, eighteen is an age of special import, for, as will be seen later, it is then that Royalty enters into majority of a limited kind, and in consequence there was a great deal of speculation about what action the King might take to mark the occasion. In many different quarters, the suggestion was mooted that His Majesty should bestow a new title on his daughter, in recognition of her new status. In Wales, where the direct connection of the Principality with the Royal House dates back for more than six hundred years to the day when Edward I made his infant son the first Prince of Wales, there was tremendous enthusiasm for a proposal that the ancient custom of reserving that title for a male heir should be waived, so that Princess Elizabeth might henceforth be known as the Princess of Wales. Welsh men and women of all degrees gave the idea their support.

Welsh M.P.s, led by Sir Henry Morris-Jones, backed the suggestion, and the local council at Pwllheli, in Caernarvonshire, went a step further by passing a resolution on August 23, 1943, asking the Prime Minister to recommend to His Majesty that the title of Princess of Wales should be created and bestowed on his elder daughter. There was, protagonists of the idea claimed, some shadowy precedent for such an act in 1525, when

A family group on an important occasion: in the grounds of Windsor Castle on Princess Elizabeth's eighteenth birthday. The Princess sits between her father and mother, with Queen Mary next to the King. Behind are the Duke and Duchess of Gloucester, Princess Margaret, the Princess Royal, the Duchess of Kent, and the late Earl of Harewood.

Princess Mary was sent to Ludlow Castle to exercise the powers of Princess of Wales, though she was never formally invested with the title.

How much, if any, of his time Mr. Winston Churchill was able to spare from his planning and direction of the war to attend to this domestic, but none the less important matter, has not been revealed, but the Pwllheli Council received a reply regretting that their suggestion was not possible.

It was not possible for exactly the same reason which rendered it impossible for Princess Elizabeth to be made Duchess of Cornwall: the Princess of Wales is a title reserved exclusively for the wife of a Prince of Wales, who must be the eldest son of the reigning Sovereign.

Eager to revive their close association with the Royal House by some other means when the first had failed, the loyal folk of the Principality put forward a new suggestion, this time that the King might create an entirely new Welsh title, and make his daughter Duchess of Cymru, thus incorporating into a Royal title the ancient Celtic name for Wales: or alternatively, Duchess of Gwalia, with the new title descending always to the eldest daughter of the Sovereign, as that of the Prince of Wales does to the eldest son.

Undoubtedly these, and all other suggestions of a sensible character—there were one or two which scarcely merited inclusion in this category—were the subject of careful attention by the King and His Majesty's advisers. One which certainly must have been numbered among these emanated from Scotland, where staunch loyalists wanted to tie yet another and a new bond between their ancient Kingdom and the Princess who one day may rule over it as part of the realm of Great Britain. They bluntly suggested that if, as seemed to be the case, she could not be made Princess of Wales because of the prior claims of a possible and as yet unborn Prince, there was nothing of that kind to prevent her being made Princess of Scotland.

It was the passing of the Regency Act of 1943, which both clarified, and in part superseded, the former Regency Act of 1937, that gave impetus to public interest in the Princess's title; and prompted so many bodies and individuals to put forward their various suggestions. The 1943 Act mentioned the Princess by name, and affected her directly, for under it she was empowered with an important and high function of State, the qualification to act as one of the Councillors of State to whom the Royal powers are delegated in the absence of the Sovereign from the Kingdom, or his inability through illness or other cause to attend to the affairs of the nation. Suddenly, people, who had been accustomed to thinking of the Princess as a little girl, a sentiment which the strict seclusion and privacy of her early upbringing had done much to foster, began to realise that she was fast growing up, and would shortly begin to take her place in public life. This, if any, was surely the time for a change in her title to be made. But, having passed all the suggestions submitted to him in careful review, having given due consideration to each, having weighed the arguments for a change, having examined all the precedents governing the case, the King, in his wisdom, decided to make no alteration in his daughter's title. It was as Princess Elizabeth that she had grown up, it was as Princess Elizabeth that the Empire and the world at large knew her, and it seemed, perhaps, too late to make a change. The suggestion that she should be Princess of Wales had been ruled out of court, the title of Princess of Scotland might have conveyed some slight and unseemly preference for one section of the United Kingdom over the others, the title of Duchess of Cymru could scarcely have recommended itself to eighteen-year-old Elizabeth, who would have had to yield up her familiar Royal title of Princess for one borne by others not of Royal rank, and there were equal objections to the various alternatives that had been put forward, so that, after the period of eager interest had passed, reflection at leisure produced general agreement that His Majesty had in this, as in so many other matters, once again correctly led and interpreted the real wishes of the nation.

So, in conformity with her own wishes, Princess Elizabeth continued to retain her single Royal title as Princess, and it was not until her marriage to Prince Philip, the newly created Duke of Edinburgh, that her title altered. To-day, her full official designation is "Her Royal Highness The Princess Elizabeth, Duchess of Edinburgh", but by her own wish, in happy accord with public sentiment, she still prefers to be known generally by the style that has become so well-known and so well-loved,—Princess Elizabeth.

Scotland was naturally delighted at the announcement of the King's choice of a Scottish title for his son-in-law. But Wales and England were not overlooked, and the Duke's second and third titles also have apposite territorial connections. He is Earl of Merioneth in Wales, and Baron Greenwich in England. His Dukedom is a Peerage of the United Kingdom, and it is as Duke of Edinburgh that he sits in the House of Lords.

Three Acts of Parliament, widely separated in time, affect, and indeed control, the constitutional position of the Princess to-day. The first is the Act of Settlement, passed in 1700, in the reign of King William III: the second the Regency Act of 1937, passed at the direct request of the King two months after his accession; and the third, the Act of the same name, passed in 1943, again as a result of a message from His Majesty, delivered to the House of Commons by the Prime Minister. It is a revealing searchlight on the integration of the British monarchy with the British Parliamentary system, that cardinal feature of our democracy which other nations find so difficult to comprehend and even more difficult to imitate successfully, that the position of the Sovereign's daughter should be dependent on votes cast in the elected House with an interval of close on two and a half centuries between them. There are other Acts of Parliament which have a direct effect on members of the Royal House, in particular the Royal Marriages Act of 1772, but these three are the chief in importance.

King James the First of "England, Scotland, France, and Ireland" was crowned King of England in 1603 after succeeding to the throne of Scotland as a baby of one year, on July 25 thirty-six years before. His accession paved the way for the Act of Union, joining the two thrones and countries into a single realm under a single Sovereign, in 1706. King James had a daughter, whose name, curiously enough, was also Elizabeth, who married Frederic V, Elector Palatine and King of Bohemia. It was their daughter, the Princess Sophia, who had married the Elector of Hanover, to whom the attention of Parliament was directed when the question of the future succession to the Crown became acute at the death of Mary II, the childless wife of William III, in 1694. The widower King showed no signs of re-marrying, the heiress-presumptive was Princess Anne, and if she died childless—as it proved she did—the line of Protestant succession seemed to be at a full stop. So Parliament, with the assent of King William, passed the Act of Settlement in 1700, setting forth specifically the line of lawful succession to the throne of Great Britain, which, it laid down, was to descend to the Princess Sophia, Electress of Hanover, and "heirs of her body, being protestants". Sophia had died before Queen Anne's death in 1714, and therefore it was her son who became the rightful King of Great Britain, as George I, and who founded the House of Guelph, re-named in 1917, by King George V, as the House of Windsor.

Another provision of the Act of Settlement was that "whosoever shall hereafter come to the possession of this Crown shall join in Communion with the Church of England as by law established".

A custom, whose exact origins seem lost in the remoteness of history, prescribes eighteen as the age at which a Royal person attains majority: but it is majority of a limited kind. Queen Victoria ascended the Throne two months after her eighteenth birthday. It was three years before she would, in the ordinary legal sense, leave her minority, yet there was no attempt on the part of anyone to set up, or even to suggest the setting up, of a Regency, as is necessary when a minor succeeds to the Throne. She began her reign as a full Queen Regnant, exercising the whole of the Royal powers and prerogatives herself.

On the eve of his eighteenth birthday, King Edward VII, then Prince of Wales, received a letter from his mother informing him that henceforth he must consider himself his own master: and that she would in future offer advice but never obtrude it; thus confirming the idea that the Heir to the Throne comes of age at eighteen.

Accordingly, newspapers proclaimed, as April 21, 1944, approached, that that day would mark the Princess's coming of age. They were only partly right. After the highest legal authorities in the country had, at the King's request, delved deeply into the problem, it emerged that from her eighteenth birthday on, the Princess would automatically become of age, if she ascended the Throne, on the exact precedent, of course, of her great-great-

Princess Elizabeth's personal standard or "banner": Clydeside shipyard men display the flag after it had been flown for the first time when the Princess launched H.M.S. Vanguard. The "cadency label" can be clearly seen.

grandmother, Queen Victoria. But, if she remained one of the Sovereign's subjects, she would not be of age until the normal twenty-one. This position involved an anomaly of a somewhat important kind, affecting the Princess's exercise of Royal functions. The Regency Act of 1937 had made provision for the uninterrupted exercise of the Royal authority during the absence of the Sovereign from his realm, through the medium of Councillors of State, to be empowered by commission of the King through Letters Patent under the Great Seal. But it expressly debarred from those in the line of succession to the Crown who would act as Councillors, any who were not "of full age". The Princess, therefore, who might become Queen overnight with full powers, could not take any share in the exercise of the more limited powers entrusted to the Councillors of State during her father's absence abroad. At once, the King took steps to have this matter put right, and sent a message to the Commons on September 23, 1943, recommending an amendment of the Act to permit the inclusion of the Princess after her eighteenth birthday.

The King's Message, read by Mr. Speaker, included this significant passage:—"The earnest desire of the Queen and myself that our beloved daughter, Princess Elizabeth, should have every opportunity of gaining experience in the duties which would fall upon her in the event of her accession to the Throne, leads me to recommend that you should take into consideration the Amendment of the Act mentioned in such manner as to provide for including among the Counsellors of State the person who is heir apparent or heir presumptive to the throne if over the age at which the accession of a Sovereign does not necessitate a Regency—namely, the age of eighteen."

At the same time, another anomaly of the 1937 Act was removed, that by which the Queen was automatically included among the Councillors of State, even when, as was the case in the Royal visit to Canada in 1939, she herself was abroad at the time with the King.

It was not long after her birthday that Princess Elizabeth had her first opportunity of exercising the powers newly bestowed on her by Parliament. Immediately before setting out on his flight to Italy, to visit General Sir Harold (now Field Marshal the Viscount) Alexander and his armies, on July 2, the King signed the Warrant under the Great Seal, appointing five Councillors of State who would carry out all Royal functions, except the dissolution of Parliament and the creation of Peers, in his absence. The five were: the Queen, Princess Elizabeth, the Duke of Gloucester, the Princess Royal, and Princess Arthur of Connaught, that is the Consort, and the four next in succession who were of age, of British nationality and domiciled in this country.

The King's nephew, Viscount Lascelles, who had celebrated his twenty-first birthday five months earlier, was compulsorily absent from the country in a German prisoner-of-war camp. His place as the fourth of age in succession was taken by Princess Arthur.

It throws a happy light on the easy intermingling of State duties and normal domestic life in our Royal family that the Princess spent her first day as a Councillor of State visiting Girl Guides at a camp in Windsor Great Park, with her sister, where they were joined in the afternoon by the Queen.

Her first actual experience of State duties came a day or two later, when, with the Queen, she signed, on behalf of the King, a commission authorising a Royal Commission, of the Lord Chancellor (Viscount Simon), the Earl of Lucan, and Lord Daryngton, to signify the Royal Assent to Acts just passed. The familiar words, "Signed by the King with his own hand" were replaced at the end of the Commission by the words, "Signed by the Queen and Princess Elizabeth". In the first days of August, with the King still away, Court Circular recorded that the Queen and Princess Elizabeth, "being Councillors of State under His Majesty's Commission, this morning received in audience Major Arthur Young, M.P. (Vice-Chamberlain of the Household), who presented an Address from the House of Commons, to which Her Majesty and Her Royal Highness were graciously pleased to make reply on behalf of the King". That was the first occasion on which Court Circular had recorded the Princess as "giving an audience". It will be noted that the Circular spelt the title as "Councillors" whereas the Parliamentary usage is the archaic form "Counsellors". Next day, in similar terms, it was announced that the Queen and the Princess had received an address from the House of Lords, presented by the Lord Chamberlain (the Earl of Clarendon), to which they also made reply on behalf of the King.

The Councillors of State are vested with the full Royal powers and prerogatives, with two important exceptions: they may neither dissolve Parliament, nor may they create peers. These two powers are reserved for the exclusive use of the Sovereign himself, since they are the two most potentially important instruments of government still pertaining to the Crown. Any one Councillor's signature on a State document carries the full weight of the deputed authority of the King, though in practice, it is customary for two to sign, as did the Queen and Princess Elizabeth in the instance cited above.

Since then, Princess Elizabeth has had no further opportunity of exercising any active part in the affairs of State. During the King's absence from the realm, in his other realm of South Africa, she was with her father and mother, so that neither the Queen nor the Heiress Presumptive were able to act as councillors for His Majesty on this occasion.

Nor has the Princess, so far, been appointed to "His Majesty's Most Honorable Privy Council", that ancient and still most powerful body, not elected by the people, but chosen by the King, whose origins go back to the "Curia Regis" of pre-Norman times, and whose dictates, the well-known "Orders in Council", ruled, under the Parliamentary authority of the Emergency Powers Defence Act, the daily lives of all the King's subjects during the war. There are precedents in plenty for the appointment of a woman Privy Councillor: several are among the three hundred odd members to-day. An heir-apparent has nearly always been made a Privy Councillor and it is reasonable to assume that the Princess will be sworn in as a Councillor some time in the future.

The King's daughter is a Princess of the Blood Royal, but not a peeress in her own right, which would seem to remove her from the disability attaching to peers of the realm, who are expressly debarred from the franchise. Whether she became entitled to the vote on reaching twenty-one is a nice question for the constitutional lawyers: but it is extremely unlikely that she will ever use it. Should the King confer a peerage on his daughter at any time, and should the existing bar on women who are peeresses taking part in the debates of the House of Lords be raised, there would seem to be no reason why Princess Elizabeth should not become the first woman to take her seat in the Lords, but that is carrying the question into speculative realms.

Since pre-Restoration days, the reigning Sovereign has been excluded from the House of Commons while in session, a right so jealously guarded by the "faithful Commons" that they take the trouble to shut the door in the face of Black Rod, the King's Messenger, when he comes to summon them to the other House to hear the King's Speech at the opening of Parliament. But the ban does not extend to the King's heir, who may listen to the Commons debates as often as he—or she—may wish. Significantly, in the plans for the new House that is to arise from the bombed and burned ruins of the old, provision has been made for a private lift to take Princess Elizabeth to her special seat in the gallery whenever she wants to hear what M.P.s are saying.

Her first official visit to the Houses of Parliament was with her father and mother, when she went to hear both Houses tender their victory congratulations to the King on May 17, 1945. She went, again in State, on October 21, 1947, to the Palace of Westminster, to take part as Heiress Presumptive for the first time in the ceremonial opening of Parliament by the King, though her part was confined to sitting on a crimson chair on the steps of the Throne, below and on the right hand of her father. On January 23, 1948, the Princess went again to the House, this time in private with her husband, the Duke of Edinburgh. They took places in the Distinguished Strangers' Gallery to hear Mr. Churchill speak in a full dress debate on foreign affairs. The Princess lunched with Mr. Speaker, and spent the afternoon listening to the debate. Her busy programme of duties prevents such visits being frequently made, but she follows the give-and-take of political debates with much closer attention than even most M.P.s suspect, reading them fully in Hansard, the official report of the proceedings in Parliament, which is sent her daily at the Palace while the House is in session.

The Royal visit to New Zealand and Australia, planned for the spring of 1949, was to give the Princess a further opportunity of participating directly in the affairs of State as a Councillor, and this time the senior Councillor, of State in the King's absence from the realm. It is a pointer to the difference in the constitutional positions of the Princess and her sister that the amended Regency Act did not bestow on Princess Margaret the same responsibility as it did on Princess Elizabeth, of acting as a Councillor of State after her eighteenth birthday. Princess Margaret cannot so act until she comes of full legal age at twenty-one.

Princess Elizabeth and her sister take a nursery ride together : in the play-room at 145 Piccadilly.

CHAPTER FOUR

The Unknown Princess

HER EARLY SECLUSION AND HOW SHE EMERGED FROM IT

FOR the first fourteen or fifteen years of her life, Princess Elizabeth lived, as far as the general public were concerned, in almost complete seclusion. This was, as has already been indicated, a result of the deliberate policy laid down by her parents, and fully approved by King George and Queen Mary, at the time of her birth. Nothing would have been easier or on the surface more beneficial to the monarchy than to yield to the popular clamour for more public appearances by the Princess, already christened "the Nation's Darling", and a series of functions attended by her as a little girl would undoubtedly have set loose a great wave of loyal, if sentimental, enthusiasm, for the Royal Family as a whole. But such a move was far from the thoughts of her father and mother. Instead, they wished to shield their daughter for as long as possible from the fierce glare of publicity that must, as they well knew, one day be turned upon her. Each and every request for the Princess's attendance at functions, no matter of what kind, no matter how worthy the cause for which they were being held, was turned down with a politely worded but firm refusal. No amount of persuasion, no inducement could be made to affect this attitude. Recognising the right of the public at home, and in the Empire overseas, to know something of how the Princess was growing up, the Duke and Duchess permitted a certain small number of authorised, official studio portraits of her on her birthdays and on other exceptional occasions, to be reproduced in the Press. But that was all. Once the first full spate of interest in her as a baby had passed, the Duke and Duchess took good care that, wherever the Princess was, at 145, Piccadilly, at Royal Lodge, Windsor, at Glamis Castle, at St. Paul's Walden, at Sandringham or at Balmoral, she should be protected from all intruders on her privacy.

This policy had the natural, though unlooked for, effect of stimulating public desire to know more about the little Princess, and all sorts of stratagems were evolved by the more determined and less scrupulous newspapers to satisfy it.

One story of the Princess's very young days both illustrates how she was early taught the importance of good manners, and shows her natural keen wits. When she was five, she had been rude one day to her governess. As punishment, it was decreed she should be "sent to Coventry" till she had apologised. Next morning, when lesson time came, Princess Elizabeth greeted Miss Crawford with her usual smiling "Good morning". There was no answer. Princess Elizabeth tried again, with a similar result. When there was no response to her third "Good morning", the Princess determined on stern measures. "Good morning," she said once again, adding this time the imperative words, "It's Royalty speaking!" When her mother heard the story, she explained that Royalty was not an excuse for bad, but carries an obligation to exceptionally good, manners, and the Princess remembered the lesson.

63

QUEEN OF TO-MORROW

The baby Princess gazes intently at the busy London streets as she is taken for a drive.

She also remembered the trick for attracting attention. A year or so later, she visited an agricultural show in the country with Queen Mary, who had requested in advance that the show people should not keep the little Princess talking too long. When she asked an old country-man exhibitor about his cattle, the old man, with Queen Mary's admonition in his mind, refused to be drawn into conversation. The Princess repeated her questions. Still there was silence. Then Princess Elizabeth decided to apply pressure. "You must answer, you know," she told the old man. "It's Royalty asking."

Another lesson of those early days which has often to stand her in good stead nowadays was to suffer boredom without showing it. This is one of the polite usages in which Royalty has perforce to be expert. Self-important local figures do not always consider the feelings of their Royal visitors when declaiming long and platitudinous speeches, but never by the movement of a muscle will Princess Elizabeth show her feelings, however impatient she may well be to proceed with her programme. It was when callers came to visit the Duchess of York at Piccadilly that the Princess had her first lessons in this difficult art. If she happened to be downstairs when the visitors arrived, she saw how her parents received them with courtesy, took her cue from them, and thus learned her first lessons in good manners. She had her natural likes and dislikes among the "grown-ups", some of whom were very boring to her childish mind, especially when their arrival chanced to interrupt some game or other, but it was in this way that she began to learn self-restraint and consideration for others, both of which qualities she possesses in a marked degree to-day.

It was in those nursery days, too, that she learned of the eager public interest in all her activities, in her private as well as her official life, which makes her so eager and so grateful for a little privacy and freedom from intrusion to-day.

Photographers in those days would conceal themselves at vantage points along the route they thought the Princess would follow when she went out for a walk, a drive, or a ride. Servants and members of the Duke and Duchess's household were bombarded by questions, but all in vain. The stratagems were met by counter-stratagems, the questions by complete unrevealing silence, until at last it became recognised, even by the most persistent, that the Princess was not to be made into a public figure yet awhile, that her childhood and girlhood were not to be spoilt by outside prying.

So well and successfully was this wise policy carried out that it was possible for the Princess and her sister—for, after the birth of Princess Margaret, exactly the same policy

Princess Elizabeth shares a joke with Princess Margaret as they sit in one of the State Rooms at Buckingham Palace. The two Royal sisters have always had the strongest affection for each other. Shelves in the corner are empty of valuable china, stored away in safety against the risks of war.

Photograph: Fox Photos Ltd.

of privacy was pursued in her case—not only to lead normal lives but even occasionally to make one of their rare appearances in public without being recognised. At such functions as the Military Tournament at Olympia, where they sat in the Royal box, or on great occasions of State, at the Coronation, at the return of the King and Queen from their Canadian tour, the Princesses were, of course, recognised, and given a particularly enthusiastic welcome by the crowds. But on other occasions, where they were not expected to be present, their attendance often passed unnoticed.

It was while the King and Queen were in Canada and the United States that this aspect of affairs became specially noticeable: and there was nothing that could have given more pleasure to their parents than to hear from Queen Mary, and from Miss Crawford, in their frequent, detailed letters reporting the Princesses' activities, that they were escaping overmuch attention from the public.

At this time, Queen Mary, much to her own pleasure, and to the delight of her grand-daughters, began to escort them on the series of visits to museums and places of historic interest mentioned in a previous chapter, and these visits inevitably meant that the Princesses were seen by more people than ever before. Queen Mary, with her characteristic consideration for others, refused to allow the public to be excluded from the galleries or museums where she was taking her granddaughters. All she stipulated was that there should be no advance announcement made to attract large crowds. People who were visiting a museum for their own pleasure or instruction, by chance at the same time as the Princesses, should not, she felt, be deprived of the opportunity of seeing them, so long as crowds of sightseers did not flock in, merely because they were there. And the surprising thing was that, at a number of these places, not only did the sightseers not crowd in, but most of the people already in the buildings failed to notice the Royal party at all.

This phenomenon was particularly marked on the day when the Princesses had the great thrill of riding in an ordinary underground train for the first time in either of their lives. Lady Helen Graham, Lady-in-Waiting to the Queen, and Miss Crawford accompanied the two Princesses, when they drove up to the imposing entrance to St. James's Park Station, headquarters of the London Passenger Transport Board, where Epstein's queer statues of Night and Morning keep watch over London's hurrying millions. No highly placed representatives of the Board were there to greet them. That would have spoilt the whole thing, by turning it into an official occasion, which was just what it was designed not to be. Instead, the Lady-in-Waiting took the four tickets, while the Princesses —then aged twelve and eight respectively—watched in wonderment as the change and the tickets appeared as if by magic, the party passed through the turnstiles, unrecognised by the busy ticket collector, who afterwards almost refused to believe that he had really seen the Princesses, and down onto the platform to await the next east-bound train. To the Princesses, it was a really exciting adventure. Everything was new to them, the advertisements on the walls, the tobacco and newspaper kiosks, the changing names on the train indicators, the bustle of passengers surging in and out of the lighted coaches, the loud voices of the porters calling the names of stations. They looked about them in wonder, asking Lady Helen quick, eager questions. It was perhaps two or three minutes before the right train came in, but in that time no one noticed the little Royal group standing on the platform. Glancing at them, a good many passers-by probably thought

*Enjoying the sunshine in an open carriage: this was a frequent childhood
outing for the two Princesses.*

"How like Princess Elizabeth that girl is", never imagining that it could possibly be the Princess herself on the underground station.

In the Inner Circle train, it was just the same. No special seats had been reserved for the Royal travellers. They sat demurely enough with their two ladies, in a third-class carriage, among other passengers, looking up at the underground maps, following the progress of the all-too-short journey, peering out of the windows as the train ran into Westminster and then Charing Cross. Here came another thrill, their first ride on an escalator, as they were led through the maze of passages and stairs to change into the Northern line for Tottenham Court Road station, where their destination was the Young Women's Christian Association headquarters in Great Russell Street. Princess Elizabeth stepped gaily and confidently onto the moving stairway, with her left foot correctly first, then turned to watch her sister, as Princess Margaret, following not quite so confidently, stepped on with wrong foot first, but quickly recovered her balance. As the Princesses with their attendant ladies went slowly down the escalator, hundreds of Londoners being borne upwards on the opposite moving staircase looked in surprise at the two demure girls, in simply cut coats and tam-o'-shanters, puzzling to know whether they could really be the King's daughters.

Not to be recognised was an added delight to the Princesses, both of whom were already familiar with their *Arabian Nights* and the incognito journeyings of Haroun-al-Raschid. To any ordinary child, to spend a day as a Princess would be a fairy story come true: and to a Princess, to be treated, and to be able to behave, for a few hours as an ordinary child, is almost equally a magical experience.

66

THE UNKNOWN PRINCESS

In the brightly-lit Tube carriage, the Princesses again amused themselves reading the station names and checking the progress of their journey—just as nearly every child does on its first underground journey. At Tottenham Court Road, the little Royal party hurried off the train and up the stairs, leaving behind them some very perplexed passengers, who went on scratching their heads and arguing if their fellow travellers had been the Princesses or not, till the question was settled by a paragraph in the morning papers, announcing that the Royal sisters had been for their first Tube ride.

After a visit to the "help-yourself" cafeteria of the YWCA, where they took cups of tea, the Princesses set out on the return journey to the Palace, descending again into the Tube station, taking tickets, changing at Charing Cross, and so arriving at St. James's Park again, where the big Royal car was waiting to take them across to Buckingham Palace. This time, things did not go quite so well. Princess Margaret, who had firmly refused to be separated from the tickets throughout the exciting journey, forgot all about such formalities as handing them over at the end of it, with the result that the ticket collector had to run out into the street and ask the small passenger for them. Then he, if no one else, was in the secret. When he returned to his post at the platform barrier, he proudly announced the identity of the ticket holders, adding that he would ask the Board permission to keep the tickets as a souvenir.

Back at the Palace, the Princesses wrote a full account of their adventures in their next letter to the King and Queen in Canada, adding, according to report at the time, a petition to be allowed soon to make their first ride in a London bus. That request, if it was ever made, was not, apparently, granted. It was not until July, 1946, that the Princesses made their first bus ride, paying fares as ordinary passengers on a country service from Dartmouth.

After that brief period of unexpected and unannounced visits to public places, including the Children's Corner at the Zoo, which passed away their spare time while their father and mother were in Canada, the Princesses reverted to their normal life of seclusion, disappearing entirely from the public gaze in August of that fateful year, 1939, when they went north to Balmoral with the King and Queen for the Court's summer stay in the Highlands, which, this year, was to be so quickly and suddenly interrupted by war, though they themselves would stay longer in Scotland than either of them ever imagined.

The King had been called to London to stay in his capital while his Cabinet Ministers and his Ambassadors waged their last desperate, unavailing fight to save peace. The Queen went South, too. To their own unconcealed delight, the Princesses remained at the Castle, "in residence" alone for the first time in their lives. As the senior member of the Royal family present, thirteen-year-old Princess Elizabeth assumed the dignity of "head of the household", for, though there were members of the Royal entourage in charge of the Royal sisters, nevertheless it was Princess Elizabeth who was the titular head of the Castle household, a circumstance that had an amusing sequel some three weeks later when the national registration for identity cards was made on Friday, September 29, 1939. Forms had to be filled in at Balmoral Castle, just as in every other house in the land, and in the list of inhabitants of the Castle on that night, the name of Princess Elizabeth was entered in its proper precedence, at the head of all the others, with that of her sister, Princess Margaret, second. All identity cards were numbered in exact accordance with the particulars given in each household, with the result that

Princess Elizabeth and her mother and sister arrive by rail for a visit to Glamis Castle.

both Princesses hold cards whose numbers start with the letter "S" denoting that the holders are registered in Scotland.

In Princess Margaret's case, this is particularly apt, since she was born in that country.

But what pleased young Princess Elizabeth more than the "S" at the beginning of her number was the figure "1" which terminated it—official proof and recognition of her proud position as (temporary) head of the household.

While the Princesses were still away in Scotland, the black curtain of security descended, forbidding all public mention of the whereabouts of the Royal family, all advance accounts of their activities. This very necessary censorship made the task of shielding them from unwanted publicity simple and automatic. Several times during that quiet halcyon period of the "phoney war", the enforced separation from their daughters tempted the King and Queen to bring their children back to London. But the Queen, whatever the promptings of her maternal feelings may have been, put, as she invariably has done, the duty of setting an example as Queen before all else, and the Princesses stayed in the country. When she went among the people, the Queen made no secret of her regret at seeing so many children back in the towns, and voiced her earnest hopes that the mothers would try to keep them out of danger—a plea that was much the more effective when the Queen could add from her very own experience, "I know how sad it is to be apart from the children: but it's best for them."

Meanwhile, preparations for ensuring the safety of the King and Queen themselves in the event of mass bombing of London had been hurried forward. In the ancient dungeons of Windsor Castle, deep underground, thick stone walls had been strengthened, sturdy roofs, built centuries before, had been buttressed, and a series of air raid shelters constructed that were as safe, even against a direct hit, as anything could be. To Windsor the Princesses travelled in great secrecy to join their parents for the first Christmas of the war and to take up those quarters at Windsor Castle which were to be their permanent home for the rest of the five years of war.

So well-kept was the secret of their whereabouts, that the enemy propaganda machine proclaimed with growing conviction that the King and Queen had sent their daughters out of the country to Canada—a sure sign, they added gloatingly, that all was over as far as the United Kingdom was concerned. Down at Windsor, the loyal inhabitants of the Royal Borough, accustomed to seeing the two Princesses on their frequent riding or driving excursions through the town, smiled at the German stories—but kept silent.

THE UNKNOWN PRINCESS

Plans, very definite, detailed, and elaborate, had, in fact, been made with the approval of the Cabinet and the military high command, for the evacuation of the Princesses if invasion should come. The safety of the Royal family if the Germans landed was a problem of paramount importance. Mr. Churchill and the members of his War Cabinet gave the matter their closest attention, and drew up a series of schemes, designed to meet different contingencies. Cars, their tanks full, their engines in race-track condition, stood in readiness, bearing secret code signs giving them absolute priority over all traffic: and Princess Elizabeth and Princess Margaret were ready at a moment's notice to leave with the King and Queen.

Princess Elizabeth spent six wartime birthdays at the Castle. It was there that she was made Colonel of the Grenadiers, there that she came of Royal age at eighteen, there that she signed her first State papers as a Councillor of State while her father was abroad, but at most a few hundred of the Windsor townsfolk had greeted her on her birthdays. By contrast, on her twentieth birthday, on Easter Sunday, April 21, 1946, thousands of loyal citizens made their way to Windsor for the holiday, eager to see, most of them for the first time, the heiress to the throne. By the King's permission, the East Terrace of the Castle, which runs underneath the windows of the Royal apartments, was thrown open to the public, and two Guards bands, those of the Royal Horse Guards, and of the Princess's own regiment, the Grenadiers, played in the afternoon. As a result, an astonishing display of enthusiasm occurred, with over thirty thousand people crowded in orderly fashion along the Terrace, cheering lustily at every interval

in the music, as they looked up to the open windows of the Royal rooms, where Princess Elizabeth sat with the King and Queen, Queen Mary, and Princess Margaret. It was a remarkable demonstration of popular affection for the Princess and her parents, the first opportunity the country had had of showing its feeling for the young Royal heiress.

When Princess Victoria celebrated her important eighteenth birthday, the last she was to spend as a Princess, at Kensington Palace, one hundred and nine years earlier, the day was observed as a public holiday from eight o'clock onwards, church bells rang at intervals in honour of the day, both Houses of Parliament observed the holiday, and that night thirty-eight public dinners, each attended by a Member of Parliament, were held, "within four hours' ride of the metropolis". At one, an M.P. uttered a sentiment which could be repeated without alteration to-day. "When, in the fullness of time,

In " Service rig " at sea: Princess Elizabeth wears a " Vanguard " ribbon.

69

As happy as " sand boys " : Princess Elizabeth and Princess Margaret with spades and buckets during a stay at St. Paul's Walden.

the illustrious Princess is called upon to ascend the Throne of her ancestors, she will, I am in my heart confident of it, obtain that best title to the Crown, the confidence, the respect, and the affections of the people."

The comparison between those rather over-formalised rejoicings of Victoria's day, and the spontaneous, unrehearsed enthusiasm of the Easter crowds on Princess Elizabeth's twentieth birthday, and the almost complete absence of ceremony on her eighteenth anniversary, is a comparison between the two ages. Imperious Victoria, even at the end of her long reign, could little have foreseen, nor would she probably much have relished, the days when the Sovereign's greatest active daily power is exercised by force of example, when the King is regarded more and more as the trustee and guardian of his people's right to their own independent democratic rule: but the warm-hearted affection of the Easter crowds for her great-great-granddaughter would have brought her real joy. It was evidence, if evidence were needed, that no matter what the changes in the political scene, no matter what further brakes a flexible constitution might put on the powers and prerogatives of the Throne, the country's love for the monarchy had not changed, but had strengthened, and become more personal with the passing of the years.

Of all the happenings at Windsor Castle during the war years, the events that immediately preceded Princess Elizabeth's sixteenth birthday would have caused Queen Victoria most surprise. On that day, the Princess, accompanied by her mother, set out from the Castle in one of the royal cars to drive to Victoria Street, where the big maroon limousine halted outside an unpretentious entrance, above and beside which several printed notices bearing the King's name were displayed. It was the local Windsor Office of the Ministry of Labour, more familiarly known as the Labour Exchange, and the King's daughter went there, as 20,000 girls of her own age were doing all over the country at their local Exchanges, to register under the National Service Act, on reaching the age of sixteen.

That procedure had been decided upon by the King for more than one reason. For the Princess to register "at home", at Buckingham Palace or Windsor Castle, would have been to give her a privilege denied to all other youthful candidates for national service: for her to have gone to the Ministry of Labour, and filled in her form in the presence of Mr. Ernest Bevin, then Minister of Labour, would have seemed too much like showman-ship, and this above all was what the King wanted to avoid. Besides these negatives, there was the positive advantage that if the Princess went to the local Labour Exchange, it would do much to remove the snobbish reluctance of many parents to let their children visit the Exchanges, which, until then, had been largely associated in the public mind with unemployment and the "dole".

When Princess Elizabeth, in the uniform of her own "pre-entry" training organisation, the Girl Guides, walked into the little, sparsely furnished Exchange where two girl clerks waited to attend her, under the supervising eye of two officials from the Ministry, a new line in British constitutional history was written. Never before had a Sovereign's daughter registered for service like any other of his subjects: never before had such a personal piece of Royal business been transacted in such an ordinary, routine fashion. The only concession made in recognition of the Princess's rank was that she came to the office before the normal opening hour, so that she and the Queen should not have to wait their turn in a queue. On the ordinary buff form "E.D. 431", the Princess wrote out particulars of herself, as required by the Registration of Boys and Girls Order, 1941 —one of the several thousand Orders in Council which her father approved in Privy Council for the wartime control of his subjects. She gave her name as "H.R.H. Princess Elizabeth", entered the word "Private" under the education question, "No" to the question "Are you attending evening classes?" and gave "Girl Guides" as her youth organisation.

The Queen watched with an affectionate smile as her daughter bent over the plain wooden counter in conversation with the girl behind it, and produced her identity card —the ordinary small buff card issued to all private citizens. Ministry officials, watching too, were surprised at the calm, methodical way in which the Princess went about her business. Her registration card, a document of history in its own right, was sent off with the other Windsor cards, to be sorted and filed at the Ministry with all the hundreds of thousands of others from all over the country, not picked out, as it might well have been, for inclusion in the Royal war archives. The King had expressed his wish that his daughter should register as a private young citizen, and the Ministry faithfully carried out his commands.

Although Princess Elizabeth did not enter any of the national war services until, at her own wish, she was commissioned in the A.T.S., her registration at sixteen was no empty idle gesture. The King was determined that no one should be able to suggest that his daughter was not doing all she should in the time of national danger, and had the Cabinet, when they came to consider the problem of the Princess's war service some twelve months later, recommended that the heiress to the Throne should join one of the services or work in a war factory, there would have been no opposition on the part of the King. In fact, the Cabinet came to the opposite conclusion, taking the view that her training for future queenship was a most important form of national service, and that the claims of her position as heiress presumptive must override all other consider-ations. She had, after all, become liable, at her birth, for national service of a highly specialised kind: to interrupt her serious train-ing for this would, the Cabinet urged most strongly, be a mistake.

Like other girls, Princess Elizabeth had her own particular war heroes and naturally was prone to ask her father if he had met any of them when he saw her on returning from his many tours of R.A.F. stations, and Army camps, or his visits to the Home Fleet. It was the Royal Air Force that for a long time held pride of place in the Princess's affections. Wing Commander Stan-ford Tuck, the famous fighter pilot who had twenty-seven enemy kills, and the double D.S.O. and the double D.F.C. to

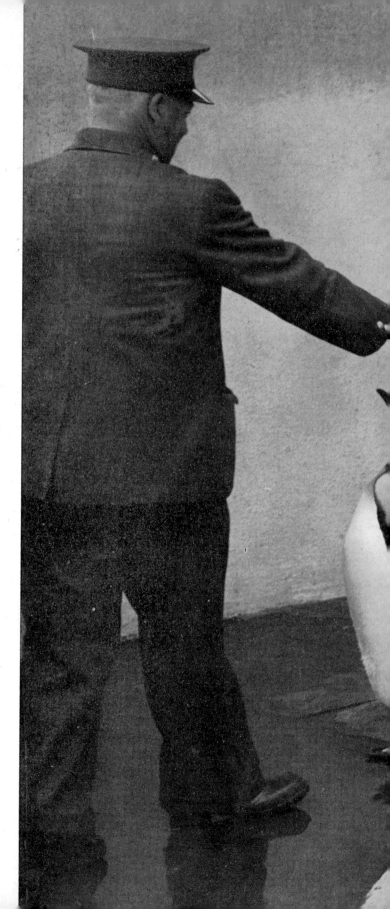

*The young Princess goes visiting : a happy
moment in the Children's Corner at the Zoo.*

The Princess plays hostess to her family—and their pets—outside her very own house, "Y Bwthyn Bach", the "Little House", given her by the people of Wales.

his credit before he was shot down in 1942 over Boulogne and taken prisoner, was one of Princess Elizabeth's early heroes, and when the King gave Tuck his bar to the D.S.O. at a Buckingham Palace investiture, he congratulated the famous ace, and told him he was very glad to see him again. "My daughter will be very thrilled when I tell her I have seen you again to-day," the King told the somewhat surprised young man, who had never even seen Princess Elizabeth in his life. "She knows all about your victories and reads every word she can about you."

Mr. Churchill, and the Admirals, Generals and Air Marshals, were familiar figures to her. She met them time and again as they came to see the King on official business, and she met, besides, all the Empire leaders who came to Britain, General Smuts, the elder statesman of Empire, Mr. Mackenzie King of Canada, Mr. Curtin of Australia, and Mr. Peter Fraser of New Zealand, as well as the chief representatives of the Allies who came here, among them Mrs. Roosevelt, who was her parents' guest at Buckingham Palace.

Apart from these personal contacts with the men and women at the top, who were directing, in greater or less measure, the whole course of the war, the Princess had no "inside information". She was not at any time allowed access to the secret papers of State, with the single exception of the short time when, in the absence of the King in Italy, she acted as one of the Councillors of State, nor did she ever know the contents of the confidential dispatches which constantly arrived at all hours of the day and night for her father's attention whether he was "on duty" in London or "on leave" at Windsor, and she kept her own maps of the various fronts, marking the Allied and German lines in accordance with what she read in the newspapers and heard on the wireless. Perhaps the King, who knew the real truth of the position at all times, good or bad, may have smiled to himself if he happened to see his daughter's maps when— as in the early stages of the Normandy invasion—the paramount need for keeping the enemy in ignorance decreed that the public at home must also be a little misled. But he certainly never ventured to alter any of the markings.

At Windsor the Princess had to be content to help on the war effort in such little ways as she could, aiding in the local salvage drive, growing vegetables and fruit in her garden at Royal Lodge, knitting comforts for the Forces. She was a constant listener to the B.B.C. news bulletins, and to the French transmissions in the European Programme.

At Windsor, too, the Princess, like other young people, learned the drill of fire fighting, practising stirrup pump exercise with her father, familiarising herself with the raid alarm procedure, and so on. She became quite expert, too, in aircraft recognition.

It was not until the Allies' "Invasion Year"—1944—that the Princess began to go about among the King's forces with her father and mother. Then, the King decided that with such epochal history in the making whose outcome must govern the shape of the world to-morrow, it was only fitting and right that his daughter, who on some morrow, near or distant, would be called into the midst of world affairs, should see something of the mighty events that were in process of formation.

One such trip took her in the Royal train to two secret encampments, where she spent two full and exciting days with the King and Queen watching battle practice by picked shock troops and armoured formations. Another memorable occasion was when she and her mother were the only non-Service spectators to witness the most dramatic pre-battle rehearsal of all time, the final practice parachute jumps and glider landings by the Airborne Division, the very tip of the spearhead of the Allied invasion. In all the long panorama of great occasions, occasions of State, occasions of national mourning or rejoicing, occasions on which she has seen, or has herself taken part in, the making of history, none can be more vivid or more enduring in the Princess's memory than that she saw in the gleaming sunshine of a summer's day in Wiltshire in the year 1944.

The Royal party spent the entire day with the R.A.F. men and their comrades of the Airborne Forces at Netheravon and nearby Bulford, inspecting airborne units, examining paratroopers' equipment, and watching a big display of formation dropping by several hundred paratroops. To Princess Elizabeth it was fascinating.

Up in the control tower of the station, with the King and Queen, the Air Chief Marshal, Sir Trafford Leigh-Mallory, C.-in-C. of the Allied Invasion Air Forces, and Lieut.-Gen. Sir Frederick "Boy" Browning, then Commander of the Airborne Troops, and now Comptroller of the Princess's Household, the Princess looked out through the observation windows at a blue, empty sky. Suddenly, with no warning, the great shape of a Horsa glider came into view, followed by another, and another, and another, till the sky, empty no longer, seemed filled with the strange, sinister craft, making their noiseless way through the air as if by magic. The first glider put down perfectly, stopped only a few yards from the Royal watchers. Close on its heels the second craft swooped down, and in a matter of minutes, the sky was empty again, the big airfield jammed with gliders, their wingtips almost touching, lined up nose to tail in long rows like so many motor-cars in a crowded park at a Cup Final.

Princess Elizabeth watched it all in silent amazement, as well she might, for nothing quite like it had ever been seen before by serviceman or civilian. It was the most astounding demonstration of mastery over the air, of precision and discipline in handling motorless planes that could be imagined. The men in the planes had bent the winds to their will like so many gods. Even as a peaceful display of gliding, it would have ranked as a wonder: the consciousness that all this was but a rehearsal for the real thing, when the pilots would have darkness and enemy gunfire to contend with besides the elements, made it all the more impressive.

Another outstanding day for the Princess was when, some time later, again accompanying her father and mother, she made a tour of four big stations of the Royal Canadian Air Force. It was an outstanding day for the R.C.A.F. as well, the first time the King had devoted a whole day to his Canadian Air Force, and the first time the Princess had visited Canadian "territory". Standing under the great wings of a dozen four-engined Halifax bombers in a hangar, the Princess watched her father decorating officers and men of the R.C.A.F. for their achievements in the D-day operations, the bombing of Caen, and in other notable air attacks. Over one hundred and fifty men from all parts of the Dominion, of all ranks from the Air Commodore from Ottawa, who headed the list, to humble aircraftsmen, received awards during the day, the names of their homes, towns and provinces, Moose Jaw, Medicine Hat, Winnipeg, Manitoba, Ontario, and so on, conjuring up a very real picture of the vast Dominion in the mind of the attentive Princess.

This was not the Princess's only experience of air stations at invasion tension. A two-day tour of R.A.F. stations and U.S.A.A.F. stations which she carried out again with the King and Queen, a month after the first landings in Normandy, has a special place in her war memories. It was the first time she had been amongst the friendly informality of the American airmen: and it was the first—and up to now the only—occasion on which she has christened an aircraft. After a night in the Royal train, the Princess drove next morning with her parents to one of the big Flying Fortress stations of the Eighth Air Force, where the Stars and Stripes flying over the buildings, the unfamiliar uniforms, the new words of command, the different method of presenting arms, helped to build up a delightful impression of freshness and novelty.

It was smiling, diminutive General "Jimmy" Doolittle, Commander of the Eighth Air Force, and hero of the first American bombing attack on Tokio, who had the pleasant task of showing the Royal visitors round the four stations they visited. At the first, the Princess had an unexpected thrill when she saw dozens of Flying Forts touching down after a highly successful raid on the German flying-bomb sites on the Pas de Calais. Then, in the middle of a crowd of cheering G.I.s, she stood with the King and Queen and General Doolittle, watching more massive formations of Forts pass overhead on their way to deliver a fresh attack on the same target. It was the boisterous informality of the G.I.s and their vociferous welcome that struck Princess Elizabeth most, in contrast to the no less eager, but more restrained and more quietly expressed welcome she was used to seeing at R.A.F. stations. And there were the cameras. Besides the large contingent of Press and Army photographers from London, half the officers and a third of the enlisted men on each station seemed to have a camera and an ambition to get a close-up

CERTIFIED COPY of an   ENTRY OF BIRTH.
Pursuant to the Births and Deaths   Registration Acts, 1836 to 1874.

B. Cert.
R.B.D.

Registration District   ST. GEORGE, HANOVER SQUARE.

Birth in the Sub-District of MAYFAIR & KNIGHTSBRIDGE in the County of LONDON

Insert in this Margin any Notes which appear in the original entry.

1 When and Where Born.	2 Name, if any.	3 Sex.	4 Name and Surname of Father.	5 Name and Maiden Surname of Mother.	6 Rank or Profession of Father.	7 Signature, Description and Residence of Informant.	8 When Registered.	9 Signature of Registrar.	10 Baptismal Name, if added after Registration of Birth.
Twenty-first April 1926	Elizabeth Alexandra Mary	Girl	His Royal Highness Prince Albert Frederick Arthur George	Her Royal Highness The Duchess of York formerly Lady Elizabeth Angela Marguerite Bowes-Lyon	Duke of York K.G.	Albert Father White Lodge Richmond Park Surrey	Seventeenth May 1926	W.R.C. Walker Registrar.	

WILLIAM R. C. WALKER, Registrar of Births and Deaths for the Sub-District of MAYFAIR & KNIGHTSBRIDGE in the County of LONDON certify that this is a true copy of the Entry No. _____ in the Register Book of Births for the said Sub-District, and that such Register Book is now legally in my custody.

WITNESS MY HAND this _____ day of _____, 192_ .

Registrar of Births and Deaths.

Princesses, like lesser folk, must have their births registered: a copy of Princess Elizabeth's certificate.

of the Princess and her parents. Overwhelming as this must have been, the King and Queen, with the Princess standing a little in the rear, took it all without demur, with the result that—if only they came out—to-day more amateur snapshots of the British Sovereign, his consort and his heiress, must grace good republican homes in the United States than are to be found in loyal monarchist homes in many nations of the British Empire.

The American airmen scored another friendly victory that day over their comrades of the Royal Air Force and the Royal Canadian Air Force alike, a victory that was a tribute to American initiative and to the democratic organisation of the U.S. Army and its Air Force. Some weeks before, when rumour said that a Royal visit was to be expected, Master Sergeant J. Gregory, hailing from Salt Lake City, Utah, had a bright idea. "Let's ask the Princess Elizabeth to name our bomber after her," said he. The wheels of officialdom began to revolve, the sergeant's idea went up through the military hierarchy till it was put before the King, who approved, with the sole proviso that the aircraft should be named not Princess Elizabeth, but "Rose of York" to maintain the rule that Royal family names are only given to ships in the Royal Navy. (*Queen Elizabeth* and *Queen Mary*, the Atlantic liners, are the only exceptions.) So it came about that it was an American, and not a British or a Canadian aircraft, which the Princess christened, and not even a new plane at that, for "Rose of York" had accomplished thirteen missions, the first of them to Berlin, before the "christening day" arrived.

Confidently, and with little trace of nerves, Princess Elizabeth smashed a bottle of British cider against the nose of the bomber, and named it. So charmingly did the Princess perform the little ceremony that a vote on that station would have nominated her the most popular person alive! When she had named "her" aircraft, the Princess shook hands with all ten members of the Fortress crew, and wished them good luck and success on all future missions. The plane ended its career in March 1945, when it failed to return from a raid on Berlin.

The Princess's first public engagement of national importance was a naval occasion, when she launched the great battleship H.M.S. *Vanguard*, the ship which later took the

Royal family to South Africa, and which was again chosen by the King and Queen for their journey to New Zealand and Australia. It was this function, which took place appropriately on St. Andrew's Day, since *Vanguard* is a Clyde-built ship, which really marked the entry of the Heiress to the Throne into national life. Princess Elizabeth seemed calm. Those accompanying her remarked on her composure. But inwardly, she was not quite so calm. When a member of the party remarked on the cold—for it was a raw November morning, with a chill breeze blowing up the Clyde—the Princess, with much feeling in her tone, replied, "I'm much too nervous to feel the cold!" Yet, when she walked through the crowds of cheering Clydesiders who had built the great warship, there was not a sign of nerves to ruffle her outward composure. She walked under the huge steel hull, more than a little awed by the gargantuan size of even the holding chains and cables which would pull up the ship when she took the water. No one of imagination can ever fail to be thrilled by the launch of a big ship. On the stocks, she seems so much dead weight, an almost immovable, certainly lifeless, mass of steel. Then, as she, slowly at first, with gathering momentum, takes the water, the ship becomes alive, the inert steel mass is transformed into an entity of grace and power and beauty.

Princess Elizabeth had heard all that long before she took her place on the flag-draped

Eleven-year-old Princess Elizabeth plants a commemoration ash tree, watched by her sister and two small friends.

THE UNKNOWN PRINCESS

launching platform, surrounded by her father's Admirals and Captains, with the First Lord of the Admiralty, Mr. A. V. Alexander, the First Sea Lord, Admiral of the Fleet Sir Andrew Cunningham (now Lord Cunningham of Hyndhope), and Lord Aberconway, chairman of the shipbuilders, at her side. With a pair of silver scissors, she cut a tape, a bottle of Empire wine smashed against the tall bows, and, in a clear firm voice that showed no trace of the nervous strain which she must have been feeling, she said: "I name this ship the *Vanguard*. May God bless this ship and all who serve in her." To the accompaniment of a roar of full-throated lusty Scots cheering, she pressed a button to set the electric launching gear in motion, and looked up expectantly at the grey stem towering above her, waiting for the miracle of ship-birth to happen.

But nothing did happen. The cheers died away. For a brief moment that seemed to stretch out in time, the ship stayed stationary. The Princess stood motionless, in a silence that was complete. Then, almost imperceptibly, the ship began to move on the stocks, the tension was over, the silence shattered by louder cheers than ever. Her face flushed with excitement and pleasure, Princess Elizabeth turned to Lord Aberconway as if to ask him if she had done her part. He shook her hand, warmly congratulating her, while the tugs took charge of the big ship. Delightedly, the Princess gazed down on the crowds of workmen and women below her, and waved her grey-gloved hand to them in a spontaneous gesture that reminded everyone instantly of the Queen.

When at the luncheon which followed Lord Aberconway presented her with a magnificent diamond brooch, shaped as the Rose of England, to be a souvenir of the occasion, the Princess said: "This will always serve to remind me that the first important public duty I ever undertook was a naval occasion." They were simple words, simply spoken, but they hit exactly the right note. Over the shipyard, the Princess's personal standard, with its white cadency label, made for her by the Royal Navy, flew for the first time: and in the hearts of the men and women, of high rank or low, who had watched her ease of manner, her friendliness, and her charm, she took her place for the first time as Princess Charming.

No greater success could possibly have been won, no one could have been more happy than the King and Queen when they heard, as they took pains that they should hear, full reports of how the Princess had fared. It was more than a personal triumph for the young Princess: it was the happiest of auguries for the future.

Princess Elizabeth was thirteen when war broke out. For another three full years, she remained out of the public gaze, continuing with her studies, her home interests, and her training, until, at sixteen, she began to emerge into the limelight. It was a gradual, carefully regulated process, so that of no single moment can it be said it was then that the Princess became a public figure. She was introduced by degrees into the fierce light (and the photographers' flashlamps) that beat on the faces of the famous. So skilfully was the transformation of the Princess-stay-at-home into Princess Elizabeth, the public figure, effected that not only were the people of the Empire prepared gently for her emergence, and given time to assess her before she took full place as Heiress to the Throne, but she herself was almost unaware of the tremendous change that was slowly but surely taking place in her life, a fact that may well account in great measure for her composure and easy presence in public to-day. As the veil was lifted more and more, first by the Princess appearing with the King and Queen at private and semi-private functions at Windsor (for example, the weekly film shows at the Castle, to which

When the Princesses went aboard the "Empress of Britain" to meet the King and Queen on their return from Canada and the U.S.A.: Princess Elizabeth shakes hands with one of the ship's officers.

troops from the neighbourhood were invited), then by her making more public appearances at ceremonies at which she was herself the central figure, and the public began to know her better, she began to fill an increasing place in the public mind and affections. Requests for her attendance at all sorts of functions, possible and impossible, began to pour into the Palace. More than once, on visits to dockyards and war factories, the King and Queen heard, to their private delight, mingled with the cheers and applause, shouts from the men—and especially from the women—war-workers, "Why didn't you bring the Princess? We want to see Elizabeth!"

But the question of the Princess's first official public tour was one not lightly to be settled. All kinds of considerations had to be taken into account. There had been repeated requests from all parts of the country to see her, there were many claims and counterclaims to be weighed against each other. Finally the King decided that the honour must go to Wales, thus fostering in a new way the ancient ties that bind the now Prince-less Principality to the throne.

Princesses do not, in the accepted sense, "come out". They do not make their début by being "presented" at Court. But the year in which her friends would be making their first curtseys in the Ball Room of Buckingham Palace, would normally be, for the heiress to the Throne, a year of crowded gaiety and entertainment, of glittering ceremonial and pomp, of theatre parties, opera visits, dances, State balls, of fashionable race meetings, picnics, horse-shows, and other social occasions of greater or less import.

Princess Elizabeth had none of this in her "débutante" year, when she was eighteen.

THE UNKNOWN PRINCESS

Instead of a background of Royal splendour, with the soft lights of the rose-crystal chandeliers in the Palace ballroom gleaming on uniforms of red, blue and gold, with exquisitely dressed and jewelled women moving gracefully through the throng, and the murmur of small-talk blending with the subdued music of a string band, she made her début in much grimmer, more realistic surroundings.

It was the vivid yellow glare of metal foundry furnaces that lit up her face in a harsh, metallic light, the deep rumble of the rolling mills that drowned her words as she met her father's subjects for the first time. In place of the white and gold walls of the Palace, she saw the high drab walls of a great metal plant, with their blacked-out windows and urgent placards begging for greater and greater efforts for war.

That was how this Princess of the twentieth century first came to the people, in the big tin-plate mills near Newport, Monmouthshire, where wiry Welsh metal workers, sweating in the hot air of the furnaces, greeted her with grins of pleasure, and cheers that could scarce be heard above the noise of the never-stopping machinery. It was a strange, moving experience the Princess will never forget.

Deliberately, and surely with great wisdom, the King had chosen this setting for the opening of his daughter's public life. No King of England has ever had a greater, deeper or more intimate knowledge of industrial Britain than King George VI. As a young Prince, he took up the study of industry and industrial conditions, then an almost despised subject, of no interest to the world of fashion; acquired, in a long series of painstaking

Sixteen years old, Princess Elizabeth registers for National Service: in Girl Guides uniform she signs her card at the Windsor office of the Ministry of Labour.

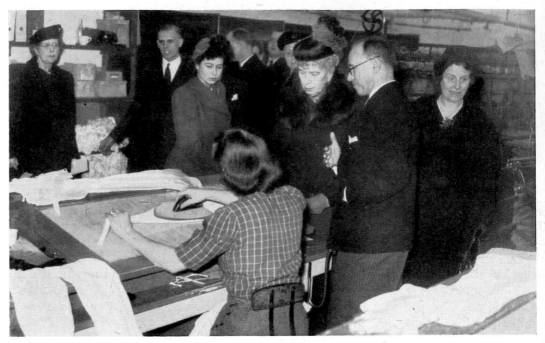

One of her first industrial visits: with Queen Mary, Princess Elizabeth inspects a factory making stockings and women's garments.

factory visits all over the country, that attracted little public attention, a vast stock of knowledge of production methods, trade customs, relations between employers, managers, and workers, and welfare schemes: and became known for his serious, purposeful interest in all industrial problems. On this solid foundation, the King went on to build up a great knowledge of the new methods of mass-production in wartime, and a valuable familiarity with the point of view of the men—and women—behind the lathes and tools and at the benches, as with the Queen he made his tireless tours of war factories and production centres. Now, when it was time for Princess Elizabeth to enter her public life the King could conceive of no better start for her than to go at once to a big works, vital to the country alike in war as in peace, and see for herself modern industry in being.

A little over-awed by the novelty of this strange fantastic world like nothing she had ever seen before, the Princess stood, in those first few moments by the furnaces, silent and absorbed, watching the quick, skilful movements of the men as they tended the swirling bubbling metal released from the foundries. Silent, too, the King, his blue-and-gold uniform as an Admiral of the Fleet turned to a queer purple and silver in the furnace glare, watched his daughter, while the foundry men, unconscious of the moment of history they were sharing, went on with their job, stopping only to throw quick appraising glances at their Royal watchers.

From that first significant factory visit, the Princess went on with her parents to other centres of war production in South Wales, to the mining valleys, the docks of Swansea, the Treforest Trading Estate, where three miles of cheering people greeted the Royal party with waving Union Jacks and the Dragon flag of Wales, and everywhere there was a special warmth in the cheers for the Princess. For eighteen years the Welsh people had waited to see the daughter of the Royal House, and what was originally designed mainly as another of the many Royal wartime factory tours was turned into a two-day progress of triumph for Princess Elizabeth. Miners, factory girls, housewives, dockers— a whole cross-section of the people of Wales-at-war turned out in thousands to see her. All through the busy two days, with every minute of the day taken up in the rapid non-stop style of the King's war tours, Princess Elizabeth remained her calm, collected self, walking always a little behind her mother and father, watching from the background as they talked to war-workers, men and women of the Civil Defence services at parades, and the regional and civic leaders of the country at official luncheons and receptions. As the Royal car drove from town to town, slowing nearly to walking pace through the crowds, the Princess sat in front of the King and Queen, smiling her thanks and acknowledging the cheers with slight bows. At several points, U.S. soldiers were in the front of the crowds, cheering as loudly as any. In several factories, she lingered alone

A visit to the Royal Tournament with her father and mother and sister in 1936.
The Queen (then Duchess of York) still wears mourning for King George V.

*Escorted by the Lord Mayor, Princess Elizabeth walks through Guildhall,
the newest Freeman of London.*

to exchange a few words with girls of her own age whom she saw at the benches and
the lathes. At one, she accepted with shy grace the bouquet proffered her by a girl charge-
hand, who told the Princess that every girl in her section had subscribed towards it.
And she did it all with such unaffected charm that the persistent Welsh, unable to hail
her officially with the titles of the Principality, bestowed on her the unofficial title of
"Ein Tywysoges"—"Our own Princess". At the end of the strenuous two days, the
Princess seemed as fresh and unfatigued as at the beginning, and when the Royal train,
on which she and the King and Queen had spent the two nights of their stay, steamed out
on its journey back to London, Wales indeed was the Princess's. She had won all hearts.

Wales was again honoured a year later, when the Princess went to Cardiff to fulfil
her first engagements alone out of London. After attending, as Commodore of the Sea
Rangers, the Council meeting of the Girl Guides Association for Wales, that night she
relaxed with two hundred Girl Guides in camp on a hillside near Cardiff. Sitting round
the camp fire with them, she joined in singing the camp songs, laughing at her own
failure to keep up with the action songs, entering into the camp spirit just as her father
used to do at his Industrial and Public School Boys camps before the war; and ate with
zest a camp supper of soup, stewed meat and trifle.

It was when she was eighteen that Princess Elizabeth made her first speech in public,
at the annual meeting of the Court of Governors of the Queen Elizabeth Hospital for
Children, Hackney, of which she had just been elected President.

Six days after her eighteenth birthday, Princess Victoria, too, made her first public
speech. But the setting and the occasion were very different.

THE UNKNOWN PRINCESS

In accordance with the ponderous custom of the day, the Lord Mayor of London went in state from Guildhall with other civic dignitaries to Kensington Palace to present congratulatory addresses to the Princess and her mother, the Duchess of Kent. After the Duchess had replied in stilted, stylised phrases, Princess Victoria spoke, in reply to the address to herself. She uttered one sentence: "I am very thankful for all your kindness, and my mother has expressed all my feelings."

The same note of genuine simplicity and sincerity rings in those few words as in the first public speech of Princess Elizabeth, more than a century later. But the modern Princess spoke for herself. Her audience of charitably-minded hospital patrons, one or two of her own older friends among them, was perhaps less awe-inspiring than the robed City Fathers who waited on the young Victoria. But she was alone, far from the familiar surroundings of her own home. The blaze of cinema lights dazzled her eyes, the whirring of recording cameras sounded in her ears as she rose to speak.

Here is the text of that, the first of the many hundreds of speeches she will be called upon to make as the years go by.

Written in advance, it bears the authentic stamp of the Princess's own phrasing, but to appreciate the proper worth of these few sentences, it is necessary to have heard the young Princess utter them in her charming, clear and well-rounded voice, to have seen her glance a little nervously round the crowded board room of the Hospital, flooded with the over-powering glare of the cinema lights (which she did not expect to be there), shrug her shoulders, make a little *moue*, then read her speech almost as easily as if she were still in her own quiet room at the Palace, rehearsing it.

The Princess said: "Lord Iliffe, Ladies and Gentlemen, I should like first to thank you all very sincerely for the kind welcome you have given me to-day as your new President —and especially Lord Iliffe and Sir Hill Child for what they have just said in proposing my election.

"I need not say how proud I am to be associated with the Hospital in this way. I feel that I have long had very close ties with it. It bears my mother's name, and my father, as Lord Iliffe reminded us, was himself President of the Queen's Hospital for many years. He was deeply interested and, indeed, one of my earliest recollections was hearing him talk of it, and of the wonderful work it was doing for children.

"I shall always endeavour to do all I can to help in the continuance of that work in the great institution which has emerged from the amalgamation of the two Hospitals. I know well how deeply interested in it are all of you who are here to-day, and what splendid service you and others are giving to it in its widespread activities. As the first act of my presidency, I should like to assure you that my own interest, and my own service, will always be given just as wholeheartedly to what we all know to be a great cause."

Simply-worded, forthright, and unpretentious, the speech obeyed the first law of all good oratory. It exactly fitted the occasion. A point that charmed the Princess's hearers was that she did not once use the formal expression of "the King and Queen", but referred to Their Majesties simply and naturally as "my mother and my father". That family note, recurring frequently in Princess Elizabeth's subsequent speeches, never fails to stimulate applause. The simple homely words ring true, warm and true, opening for a moment a window into the happy family life of the British monarchy, with an effect that the cold terms of the Royal titles could never have. Once, on an occasion of much deeper significance, later on in the Princess's career as a speaker, she was called upon to make the main speech of the day at a ceremony of great national importance. This time, the speech had been carefully prepared for her, for much of what she had to say referred to technical matters of which she had little knowledge. It was a long speech, and, of necessity, rather devoid of human interest. Going over it beforehand, the Princess decided on two minor-seeming, but important, alterations. Instead of using the formal phrase, "Mr. Chairman" at the opening, she substituted the name of the gentleman concerned, making the whole speech sound more personal. Then at the end, in a reference to the fact that the King, as a qualified Service pilot—he passed his tests in the early days of the R.A.F. at the end of the 1914–18 war—wears the winged badge of the Fleet Air Arm pilots on the sleeve of his Admiral's uniform, the original draft had the phrase "His Majesty the King". When she came to this point, the Princess said merely "My father"—and her audience, up to then a little apathetic, broke into cheers and clapped at the human touch.

It is almost an unwritten law in the Royal family not to make extemporary speeches, since Royal sayings, if not carefully thought out, might easily be subject afterwards to misconstruction. But with the help of a first-class memory, she can—and does—"read" her speeches with only occasional glances at the manuscript, thus giving, as experienced Parliamentary orators well know, the effect of spontaneity and freshness, and adding

The Royal sisters meet: Princess Elizabeth drove to London Airport to welcome her sister when Princess Margaret flew back from a visit to Ulster.

greatly to the lively interest of the speech. Now and then it happens that there is an unexpected call for a speech which cannot possibly be prepared in advance. When this happens the Princess is always equal to the occasion. With perhaps only two or three short sentences, spoken easily and with sincerity, she meets the demand, and charms the hearts of her hearers, where a long speech in stilted phrases, or a short one spoken with hesitation, would be equally wrong. That is an ability which sounds easy to acquire, but is not, especially for one accustomed to speaking from manuscript—as again a good many M.P.s could testify!

The Princess's prose style, as reflected in her speeches, is direct, free from affectation and innocent of florid imagery and phrasing. She has read extensively most of the great masters of public speaking, from Demosthenes to Burke, listened to, or read, all the great war speeches of Winston Churchill and President Roosevelt, and, in addition, has as a background her extensive reading of the great classic English writers, which, with a natural gift for clear expression, enables her to say what she wishes, crisply and clearly, without waste of words. And, no matter what the occasion, whether it be the launch of a great ship, or merely a meeting of the Girl Guides, she takes equal care and trouble over her speech, both in preparing it and delivering it.

Her first speech in public, her visit to Wales with her parents, marked the end of her seclusion. Those sequestered days were gone, and the more the people saw of her, the more popular did she become. Scotland had its first official sight of the Princess six months after Wales, when, accompanying the King and Queen on their way south from Balmoral, she spent two days in Edinburgh, visiting Service clubs, schools and factories.

Ulster, as eager as Wales or Scotland to greet the heiress to the throne, had to wait to see her until 1945, when she came with the King and Queen on their victory visit to Northern Ireland. This time, at the last moment, plans for a sea crossing had to be abandoned, and the Princess made her entry into Northern Ireland by air. It was her first flight, and the first time that a British sovereign, his consort and his heir, had travelled together by plane.

They made the flight together in a single plane, an arrangement that would have shocked the timid Ministers of an earlier day, who even felt compelled to venture a mild protest to Queen Victoria at the proposal to send both sons of the Prince of Wales together on a cruise in the *Ophir* on the score of danger to the security of the succession!

A silver-bodied Dakota aircraft, guarded by two squadrons of Mustang fighters from a Polish R.A.F. wing, four Stirling bombers, and two Warwick aircraft of the air-sea rescue service, carried the Royal passengers, and the Princess, in her A.T.S. uniform, left no doubt in the minds of anyone at Long Kesh Aerodrome, where the two-hour flight from Northolt ended, that she had enjoyed every minute of the trip. Next day, with the shouts and cheers of the Ulster loyalists ringing in her ears, the Princess went to Stormont, where the King opened the new session of the Ulster Parliament. In the Commons Chamber—used for the day by the Senate—she left her parents, to sit in the gallery beside the Speaker's Chair and watch, but take no part in, the elaborate ceremonial of the Royal opening.

Five thousand war workers met the King and Queen and the Princess at a party in the Botanic Gardens, and it is no disrespect to the King and Queen to say that Princess Elizabeth was the main centre of interest to most of those present. She left the party to attend alone an informal reception for members of the three women's services—an instance

The Princess takes her mother for a drive in her phaeton in Windsor Great Park.

of the gradualness with which the Princess has so successfully been brought into public life, first merely accompanying the King and Queen to various engagements, then carrying out a single engagement on her own in the midst of a visit by them, and finally, going about the country on her own.

The record of Princess Elizabeth's public engagements since her eighteenth birthday clearly demonstrates this gradual development of her life in public. From April 21, 1944, till the end of the year, her appearance alone in public without her parents numbered eight: in 1945, the number rose to thirty: and that same number had been reached long before 1946 had half run its course: sometimes at the rate of four in a week, with youth parades and services nearly every weekend.

Each year, in May, one afternoon is set aside to attend the annual court of governors of the Queen Elizabeth Hospital for Children, Hackney; another is booked for the annual meeting of the National Society for the Prevention of Cruelty to Children—the Princess is President of both bodies. The autumn concert and prizegiving of the Royal College of Music is another regular item on her yearly list of engagements. Again, she is President of the College, which was, indeed, the very first adult public position which the King allowed her take up, by reason of her own great and abiding interest in music, as, on her twelfth birthday, he had allowed her to be made President of the Children's League of the Princess Elizabeth of York Hospital for Children at Shadwell, now a component member of the general Queen Elizabeth Hospital for Children.

THE UNKNOWN PRINCESS

A.T.S. passing-out parades, youth organisations, especially the Girl Guides, occur frequently in the lists of her engagements. When civic authorities approach her with plans for a visit, she insists that local contingents of all the young people's organisations shall, as far as possible, be included in the programme. When there is any question of preference for the choice of a guard of honour, or other special duty near her, it is the Girl Guides who get the Princess's vote: for they were her own organisation as a girl.

Thus Princess Elizabeth in her public life shows two of the outstanding qualities of her personality, loyalty and steadfastness. She is not, and never has been, a person who takes up interests lightly, only to drop them just as easily a few weeks later. If and when her interest is aroused, she goes into whatever subject it is with thoroughness and application: and her interest is not allowed to wane with the passing of time or the claims of other new matters on her attention. To do this successfully requires a keen and retentive mind, and an ability to dispose well of time, both of which accomplishments Princess Elizabeth has already shown she possesses in so marked a degree as to bring the figure of her never-hurried, always interested, widely and deeply read grandmother, Queen Mary, vividly to mind.

Early among the Princess's public activities came visits to factories, particularly those where a great percentage of the workers are women. These visits, unquestionably, afford splendid opportunities for contact between the Princess and her future subjects which would be difficult, if not impossible, to arrange otherwise. They are the outcome of plans made for the Princess by the King, prompted by recollections of the invaluable apprenticeship to industrial knowledge he served himself visiting factories as President of the Industrial Welfare Society. Like those early visits of the King's, the Princess's visits to factories are, with set purpose, run on workaday lines, with a minimum of formality. Red carpets *do* tend to appear on stairways, flowers are apt to be massed at entrances, floors, walls and benches are at their cleanest and tidiest, but the work of the factory goes on without interruption—or at least with no more interruption than is caused by natural curiosity—while the Princess is there, for the whole idea is for her to see things as they are in everyday guise, and not to be shown a series of idealised set-pieces. Indeed, for her own part, there is no doubt the Princess would prefer all formalities and red carpets to be done away with on these occasions, though she realises that in practice that is asking the impossible.

The first of these visits was to a big modern stocking factory at Baldock: the next to the giant Battersea power station whose twin towers dominate the skyline to the south-west if you look—as Princess Elizabeth has often looked—at London's vastness from the roof of Buckingham Palace; the third to the General Electric Company's research laboratories at Wembley; and many others since have helped to give the Princess an ever-widening picture of the industries of Britain.

Partnered by a young officer of the Guards, smiling Princess Elizabeth shows how much she enjoys dancing.

CHAPTER FIVE

The Princess Off-Duty

HOBBIES AND AMUSEMENTS

WHATEVER Princess Elizabeth may owe to Queen Victoria in her mental make-up, or to Queen Mary in the perfection of her physical colouring, it is from her great-grandfather, King Edward VII, that eager lover of life, that successful master of the difficult art of combining kingship with common humanity, that she inherits her love of two of her greatest outside amusements, the theatre and racing. Neither her grandfather, King George V, who used to complain that he could neither see nor hear from the Royal box where he had always to sit when he went to the play, nor her father ever showed much serious interest in the theatre. And for both King George V and his son the Royal racing stud has lacked that deep personal interest that King Edward maintained throughout his life—often, in his earlier days to the considerable annoyance of his mother, Queen Victoria—in all matters connected with racing. Judging by the indications she has given up to now, Princess Elizabeth seems likely to follow his example in both these spheres. Before she was old enough to go on a racecourse, the Princess used to follow keenly the progress of her father's horses, and when the King's much fancied colt, Big Game, failed to win the Derby at Newmarket in 1942, nowhere was there keener disappointment than in the Royal schoolroom, where Princess Elizabeth, then 16, heard the result from the wireless. As for the theatre, her early career as a successful producer of and player in pantomimes gave a clear pointer to where her interests would lie.

Since she began to go about on her own, Princess Elizabeth has amply confirmed both these early indications, and both the racing world and the world of the theatre are delighted to welcome her as their newest Royal patron.

Her first visit to a racecourse was appropriately to the Royal course at Ascot, where she went with her father to one of the wartime "austerity" meetings, that is to an ordinary race meeting run by the Jockey Club on the famous course which they leased for the purpose from the King, and not to a real Ascot "garden party" meeting with its fashion parade and its exclusive Royal enclosure. When Princess Elizabeth went to her first Ascot, on Whit Monday, May 21, 1945, the Royal lawn was open to the public. Men and women in service uniform, war-workers in tweed coats and grey flannels, and women in trousers, American soldiers of every rank from generals to G.I.s, men and women from the Dominion Forces, and from the armies of the allies, walked in the holiday crowds in front of the bow-fronted Royal box. But it was the racing, and not the crowds, which the Princess had come to see, and she very soon made it obvious that her attention was centred on the horses, following the races through binoculars, asking questions of her father, of the Duke of Norfolk, and of Captain Moore, manager of the King's thoroughbred stud. Then she walked down with the King through the crowds to see the horses saddled and the jockeys

Princess Elizabeth, a good shot with a sporting rifle, takes some practice aboard H.M.S. Vanguard on the way to South Africa.

mounting. This was something she already knew a good deal about, for horse riding has been one of her keenest hobbies since her first lessons on the Shetland pony her grandfather gave her for Christmas when she was four, and she not only rides well both side-saddle and astride, but is thoroughly competent to groom and saddle her own horse—as she frequently used to do.

To see the gaily-coloured jockeys perched high in their stirrups cantering purposefully down the course was a new thrill for her, and she remained in the front of the Royal box for the rest of the afternoon, watching every race until the time came for her to go home with her father to Windsor.

Next race the Princess saw was the Derby. It was a wartime Derby, though peace in Europe had already come, and instead of the real Epsom atmosphere that makes the great race one of the most outstanding experiences in the sporting world, she saw it in the tamer conditions of Newmarket, with no Tattenham Corner to trap the unwary, no costermongers on their barrows, no gipsies ready to foretell any amount of future events except the result of the race, none of the trimmings of Epsom. But still it was the test of the fastest and finest three-year-olds in the country, and the rapt expression on her face as she watched the hard fought finish, with the favourite Dante winning by two lengths from Midas told anyone who cared to look—and there were not a few who turned their glasses on the Royal box—that she was enjoying the experience to the full.

These two visits made racing folk hope that the Princess was going to follow their sport. The next two made them sure she was. Crowds at Ascot in the paddock, watching the horses and jockeys preparing for the £1,000 Queen Mary Stakes, noticed a girl in khaki A.T.S. uniform in the saddling ring—and the news spread that the Princess was there. Actually, she had arrived on the course alone some time before, but scarcely anyone had noticed her in the Royal box. It was her first visit alone to the races, and this time she was determined to see everything for herself. After one race, she was granted a privilege given to few women in the history of British racing, entry into the weighing room, the most jealously guarded place on a racecourse. She watched the jockeys being weighed in, highly amused to catch their looks of unbelieving surprise as they came, tired and sweating, their racing saddles under their arms, into the room to find a woman present. It was an experience neither they nor the Princess will ever forget. When she went again to Ascot, this time with her father, she clenched all arguments about the genuineness of her interest in racing by staying on alone when the King left after the second big race. She saw two more events, leaving just before the last race on the card, and then only because the police warned her that the crush of cars afterwards would be so bad they might have difficulty in clearing a way for her.

She has been alone to Newmarket, to watch the Royal hopes for the Classics at exercise on the Heath at the chilling hour of six a.m., afterwards attending the bloodstock sales, and then being on the course in time for the first race, and she has seen racing in South Africa, and in France.

Her two visits to Newmarket races, coupled with an Easter Saturday visit to Hurst Park with the King, and her visit to the 1946 Oaks at Epsom with her parents, caused some superstitious racing folk to regard the Princess as a "luck-bringer". When she went to Newmarket in October 1944, they noted, the King's filly, Hypericum, won the Dewhurst Stakes. At Hurst Park, when she was with the King, Hypericum was beaten, but at Newmarket, with the Princess watching, again on her own, Hypericum carried off the One Thousand Guineas. When she went to her first Epsom, with the King and Queen, Hypericum was much fancied. But she could only finish fourth.

Princess Elizabeth herself has no such superstitions, and when her friends told her of the "luck" story, she just laughed. Her interest in racing is, indeed, centred on the horses themselves, their breeding and performance, and the skill and endurance of the jockeys, not on the financial results of a race. It is, however, freely stated in racing circles that the Princess usually has a bet on any big race she is watching, especially if there is a Royal entry with a chance: but her bets are by no means big ones.

Racing folk talking to the Princess have been surprised at the depth of her knowledge of bloodstock and breeding. When she went to the circus, too, she astonished the Mills brothers, who showed her round their stables, by recognising every breed of horse they had, with the single exception of a pair of Friesian blacks, a rare breed, not often seen in this country outside the circus. That is merely one more instance of her thoroughness and capacity for taking pains. When as a very young girl she began to be interested in the horses in the Royal Mews, she started to read all the books she could find pertaining to the subject, and to-day her knowledge in this respect, as in others, is wide and deep.

The Princess with her favourite pony.

About to set off on a morning ride:
the Queen sees her daughter off.

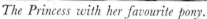

Though she is a first-class horsewoman herself, with an excellent seat and "easy" hands, the war robbed her of much opportunity for hunting and she has only once ridden to hounds, with her cousin, the Duke of Beaufort's, pack, in the winter of 1943. Those who rode with her reported she had perfect manners in the field, took her fences boldly and well, kept up with hounds, but never attempted to overrun them. Most of her riding is done within the grounds of Windsor, Balmoral or Sandringham, often, when he is free, with the King, at other times with her sister Princess Margaret. On these occasions, both Princesses wear fawn jodhpurs, coats, and a silk scarf round the head.

Like all other horseriders, Princess Elizabeth has an occasional spill: but they are few and far between, and only once has she been prevented from fulfilling an engagement because of a riding mishap, when both her legs were badly bruised after she had been thrown from her horse against a tree at Balmoral in 1945.

Besides being a good rider, the Princess is a skilful and expert driver—an ability she put to good use when to save petrol during the war she and her sister did nearly all their journeys about Windsor in a pony cart. Twice she won cups in the private driving class at the Royal Windsor Horse Show in successive years, first driving her dun-coloured Norwegian pony "Hans" in a smart black pony phaeton which had belonged to Queen Victoria, with Princess Margaret as her passenger, and next year, with her Blackfell pony "Gipsy" and a red and cream turn-out that was very attractive indeed. On both these occasions, the King and Queen were spectators, and the King's keen eye was a guarantee, if one was needed, that the Princess won her events on merits and not by

THE PRINCESS OFF-DUTY

favouritism, the slightest suggestion of which would have called forth a severe Royal rebuff. In the second year, the Princesses, competing against each other in another class, were both unplaced.

In most informal, outdoor pictures of Princess Elizabeth, you will see a small, smooth-coated dog with her. It is either Crackers or Sue, the present-day successors of Duke and Jane, her first pets, and, like them, pure-bred Welsh Corgi terriers, a faithful, intelligent, companionable breed which the Princess's choice did much to make popular.

Chin, a shaggy-haired white dog of a much rarer breed, completes the Princess's "household" of pets. He is a Tibetan lion dog, which she has had since he was a tiny puppy.

Among her other athletic interests, swimming finds a high place. She learned when she was very young, won the Children's Challenge Cup at the Bath Club when she was eleven, and gained their Life Saving Certificate. Four years later, she was the first candidate to gain the Royal Life Saving Society's artificial respiration award. At Buckingham Palace, not long before the war, the King had a private swimming pool built for her and Princess Margaret on the site of the old real tennis court. A German bomb destroyed it completely on November 1, 1940, and repairs are still a long way down the list of Royal priorities, but at Windsor there are plenty of opportunities for swimming.

Shooting is another of her outdoor interests. To the delight of the ghillies at Balmoral, it is the difficult and arduous art of deer-stalking that she most enjoys, with its long

Princess Elizabeth is a lover of the piano: the Queen and Princess Margaret listen as she plays.

A picture that shows the easy seat and good style of the Princess as a horsewoman.

days on the hillside. She shot her first stag in September 1942, bringing down three in her first day's stalk, but she has still to attain the stalker's ambition of a Royal—a stag with twelve-point antlers.

First intimation the outside world had of Princess Elizabeth's interest in the theatre was an unheralded announcement that she had been with her sister and her own young lady-in-waiting, the Hon. Mrs. Vicary Gibbs, to the evening performance of Terence Rattigan's comedy *While the Sun Shines* on November 12, 1945. She had, of course, been to the theatre many times before,—she saw her first matinée, a fairy play, *Ever So Long Ago*, as a girl of nearly eight, with her mother at the Cambridge Theatre—but always with her parents. For her to go out alone in the evening was a new departure, and next day it was front-page news both in this country and in America, especially as there were four young Guards officers in her party in the fourth row of the stalls. That visit was the forerunner of many, and the catholicity of the Princess's taste in plays can be judged by the list of the first nine or ten she went to: Noel Coward's comedy *Private Lives: Duet for Two Hands*, a "thriller": *The Years Between*, a post-war problem play: Coward's musical show revue *Sigh No More:* Cicely Courtneidge's comedy *Under the Counter:* Ivor Novello's romantic *Perchance to Dream:* Wilde's *Lady Windermere's Fan: The Sleeping Princess Ballet* at Covent Garden: *The Hasty Heart:* and *The First Gentleman*, the play about her own ancestor George IV. Since then she has seen scores of other plays. And when she went to a matinée for King George's Fund for Actors, and the organisers

A charming study in colour of the Princess in her rooms at Buckingham Palace. The platinum bracelet which she always wears can be plainly seen.

Photograph: Studio Lisa.

asked her what she would prefer to see from the Old Vic repertoire, she surprised everyone by asking for Sophocles' tragedy *Oedipus* and Sheridan's comedy *The Critic*, both *pièces de théâtre* representing a connoisseur's choice.

When Princess Elizabeth goes officially to the theatre, tradition demands that she shall sit nowhere save in a box. But when she goes in private, and is free to sit where she likes, she emphatically refuses to use a box, preferring instead to sit in the stalls, usually the fourth or fifth row. In spite of the greater privacy which a box affords—for you have only to sit back in the intervals, and no one will know you are there—the Princess likes the stalls, where literally anyone may rub shoulders with her party, because she goes to the theatre to see the play, and, like many other theatre-lovers, she claims that from a box you cannot see the play as it is meant to be seen, since at best you have only a one-sided view of the stage.

Whether she goes officially to a special performance, or privately to an ordinary show, the Princess and her party always pay for their seats. So, incidentally, do the King and Queen, the only exception being the annual Royal Variety Performance, when Their Majesties are the invited guests of the Variety Artistes Benevolent Fund, which promotes the show.

A supper party at the ball: Princess Elizabeth talks to friends across the table, while the Duke of Edinburgh makes Princess Margaret smile.

With her mother and sister she goes to the play: for her private theatre visits, the Princess prefers the stalls, but this is an official occasion, demanding a box.

For various reasons, the Princess does not like giving much advance notice of her private theatre visits, a habit which has more than once caused the managements of very successful shows to be hard put to it to find her the seats she wants. On one occasion at least, when the telephone call came through from Buckingham Palace to the manager's office in the morning, there was, literally, not a single seat unsold in the house. Some *might* be returned before evening, but that chance was too slender to be taken. So a harassed manager sat down to telephone everyone he knew personally who had seats for that evening, to ask them to put off their visit for the Princess to have their seats. . . . It took him an hour's hard telephoning, but the seats came back, and the Princess and her friends saw the show.

Another real "last-minute" visit was when the Princesses, who had already been to see Cicely Courtneidge in *Under the Counter* on their own persuaded the King and Queen to take them again, only a couple of hours before the show began. An equerry rang the theatre from the Palace rather anxiously, but this time luck was in, as two boxes were to be occupied by friends of the management. They came the following night.

Nothing has given greater pleasure to managers, actors and actresses, playwrights and playgoers alike than the Princess's keenness on the theatre, and she has won herself a place in the hearts of yet another section of the community by the absence of fuss or ceremony with which she goes to the play. One night, sitting in the stalls, a bride and bridegroom on honeymoon did not know the Princess was sitting next to them until the interval, and often the cast themselves do not know she is coming until the curtain has gone up. For her part, the Princess would be pleased if no one at all knew in advance of her theatre visits. She regards them, rightly, as part of her private life, and accordingly does not welcome unnecessary publicity, though of course she is well aware that the fact that she has been to see a play is a valuable advertisement for it, and therefore does not mind her presence being announced afterwards.

With a natural sense of rhythm, cultivated in a long series of lessons in every kind of dancing which began when she was a very small girl, it is not surprising that Princess Elizabeth is extremely fond of dancing. Fox-trots, tangos, rhumbas, old-fashioned waltzes, all come equally easily to her, and to watch her tread the intricate steps of a Highland eightsome reel to the skirling music of the bagpipes is to see dancing really enjoyed. With a complete mastery of the steps and patterns of the reel, the Princess will aid a

Her first race-visit with her fiancé. The King with his two daughters and Lieutenant Mountbatten enter the Paddock at Ascot.

What was the clown doing? Princess Elizabeth enjoys the joke in the ring at Bertram Mills' circus under the "big top" at Reading.

less-expert partner confidently through his paces, keeping the whole set going, her face flushed and smiling, her movements rapid, graceful, exact and controlled, till she imbues everyone with her own spontaneous enthusiasm, and even the watchers by the side of the floor are beating time with her. She and her husband dance particularly well together.

When she went to her first charity dance, the Princess asked for two reels to be included in the programme, and had the King's Piper from Buckingham Palace to play them, with the result that next day, fashionable dance teachers were invaded by scores of young men and women, all anxious to learn the reel, which by no means all the teachers were entirely familiar with themselves! Since then the Scottish dances have been included in the programme whenever she goes to a ball.

At private dances, particularly when it is a dance given for her at Buckingham Palace, or Windsor Castle, the Princess loves to lead a "Conga", the long line of dancers following her through the red-carpeted corridors and State apartments as the music wanes and waxes.

At one dance, Princess Elizabeth was enjoying herself so much that when the time came for the band to go home, she prevailed on her cousin, Captain the Hon. Andrew Elphinstone, who is an excellent pianist, to play for half an hour extra so that dancing might go on.

Apart from the Princess's own friends and acquaintances, quite a number of other folk have danced with her, including many Service officers, a sprinkling of Americans among them, who were invited to some of the wartime parties at Windsor Castle. One of the first partners she had outside her own circle was a sixteen year old drummer boy who boldly asked her to dance a fox-trot on the evening of her sixteenth birthday, when, with the King and Queen, she paid a surprise visit to the Sergeants' Mess of the Grenadiers at Windsor Barracks, after being made Colonel of the Regiment that morning. Once a year, too, servants at the Palace have the chance of dancing with the Princess, when, again with her mother and father and sister, she attends the Christmas ball in the Servants' Hall. Old-time numbers, like the Valeta, the Palais Glide, and the St. Bernard Waltz are apt to appear on the programme at this function, but the Princess knows, and dances, them all.

Her favourite dance numbers vary with the taste and fashion of the moment, with one or two tunes with permanent places in her favour. These include "Night and Day", "Let's Fall in Love", and the modern version of "Sur Le Pont d'Avignon".

Noticeably absent from the list of the Princess's evening amusements is the cinema. Yet she has seen most modern films, and is well conversant with the current stars of Hollywood and the British studios, a paradox explained by the fact that at Windsor

Princess Elizabeth and her fiancé dance together : at an Edinburgh ball.

Princess Elizabeth, life-saver: at a Bath Club Children's Competition which she won.

The Princesses learned to cycle when they were very young. Princess Elizabeth's machine bears evidence of a recent crash, proving that even Royal cyclists must keep control.

Castle there is a fully-equipped projector and screen, where nearly every week there is a private showing of the latest films often before their public release, for the Royal family and their guests, a sort of modern version of the "Command Perform-ances" with which Queen Victoria used to entertain her Court when she was young.

At their new home in London, Clarence House, the Princess and the Duke have a cinema of their own, too, one of the most modern projectors and sound installations, which was a wedding present from the Earl and Countess Mountbatten of Burma.

The Princess is interested, too, in amateur cine-photography. She has a camera of her own, spools from which, recording family activities of the King and Queen and Princess Margaret, would command their own price in Hollywood. But they, of course, are for private ex-hibition only. Probably the most historic film the Princess has taken is the one which she "shot" on VJ Day from the crimson-hung balcony of Buckingham Palace. Unguessed at by the massed crowds below chanting "We want the King, We want the King . . ." the Princess stood a little concealed in the long windows, filming the scene around the Victoria Memorial and along the Mall. It is the first film of a great national celebration ever to be taken by a member of the Royal family from the Palace itself.

Of more serious amusements, music ranks easily first with the Princess. She plays the piano with real skill and a natural talent that she has encouraged by years of constant study and practice. The Princess sings, too, in a pleasant, well-modulated, true voice of moderate volume and pleasing tone, delighting most in old English and Scottish songs, which she learned at her mother's knee. She revived the fashion for old English madrigals, when with her sister she arranged a weekly series of parties at the Palace, at which a number of her friends with good voices join in the singing of old traditional airs like "Greensleeves", "Blow, Blow Thou Winter Wind", and other Shakespearian songs, with Dr. Harris, the organist from St. George's Chapel, Windsor, conducting. To-day, when opportunity permits, she still joins in the Thursday evening song parties at her parents' home. Bach, Chopin, Beethoven and the other great masters of the past,

Bartok, Ravel, Delius, and the leading modernists, all are the Princess's familiars. It is from her mother, who played the piano and the harp as a small girl, that she inherits her love of music, and it was the Queen who first instilled into her small head, then covered with fair curls, the beginnings of musical knowledge and appreciation.

It was, therefore, as an expression of her genuine interest in and love of things musical that Princess Elizabeth accepted as her first fully fledged public post that of President of the Royal College of Music in October 1943. To show that it was no sinecure appointment which she had taken up, but one in which she meant to take a practical interest, she went to the Jubilee Concert of the College shortly after her appointment, to present the prizes and certificates to winning students, while the Queen watched from the centre of the balcony. This was her first experience of distributing prizes, and it was also the first time she had carried out a public engagement under the eyes of her mother, so it was no wonder that at first the Princess, standing a little shyly in her lonely eminence on the red-covered dais, was considerably more nervous than any of the young men and women students who filed past her. But her nervousness lasted for only a very short while, and after half a dozen or so had shaken hands with her and taken their prizes, she found herself quite at ease. Since then, the Royal President has continued to take an active interest in all the affairs of the College.

Another illustration of her love of music lies in her acceptance of an honorary degree from the University of London. Royalty, in common with distinguished figures in many different fields of human activity, sometimes receive academic honours qualifying them as Doctors of subjects about which they know but little. D.Ll.'s (Hon.) to whom the law is a closed book, and D.Litt.'s (Hon.) who have read neither widely or deeply, are not unknown. In this, as in so many other matters, Princess Elizabeth has taken her own independent line. It was the cap and light blue gown of a Bachelor of Music which she accepted from her great-uncle, the Earl of Athlone, Chancellor of the University, at the ceremony in the Senate House, and though she had passed no examination for her honorary degree, she could legitimately feel that she was sailing under no false colours in accepting it, for, had she been permitted by circumstances to study at a University, music would undoubtedly have been one of her chief and favourite subjects.

Whatever the Princess takes up becomes, overnight, a fashion of the day. Yachting folk hope that acceptance by the Princess and her husband of a "Dragon" class racing yacht from the Island Sailing Club at Cowes may mean that they will take an active interest in the sport, thus leading to a revival of popular interest in sailing and yacht racing.

A Royal Aladdin and Princess Roxana. The Princesses pictured after their second Windsor pantomime.

CHAPTER SIX

The Fairy Tale of Windsor

WHEN "PRINCE CHARMING" WAS A REAL PRINCESS

WHEN Shakespeare wrote, sighing for the impossible, "a kingdom for a stage, princes to act, and monarchs to behold the swelling scene," it was of the high drama of Agincourt he was thinking. Four centuries later, at Windsor Castle, the dramatist's dream of the unattainable came to reality, though it was no high drama, but a Christmas pantomime, which brought the heiress of England and her sister on to the stage, and set the Sovereign of England and his consort laughing in the stalls.

For four years running, from 1941 to 1944, Princess Elizabeth and Princess Margaret helped to write, stage and produce a pantomime each Christmas, playing the leading parts themselves, and the story of these, surely the most astonishing pantomimes that have ever been staged, is itself rather like a fairy tale, though a fairy tale in reverse, with the real Princess revelling in the part of Principal Boy, instead of the young actress dreaming of the delightful life she would lead if she were a real and not a stage Princess. It began with the erection of a stage at the Castle for the use of various artistes whom the King summoned to Windsor to provide entertainment and relaxation for his family and for the many Court officials, clerks and servants evacuated there from London, and unable to get to theatres or cinemas. Into Princess Elizabeth's fertile mind, as she talked to the famous players whom she met after their performances, came the idea of giving an entertainment herself with Princess Margaret and some of their friends, the kind of idea that many people get after watching a good show—and then do nothing about it. But with the Princess it was different. She is a firm believer in putting thought into action and within a few days, when she had secured her father's permission, plans were being discussed, Castle officials consulted, rehearsals arranged. That first show in 1940 was a simple nativity play in which the two Princesses sang.

It was such a success that Princess Elizabeth decided on a more ambitious scheme for the next year, and determined to have a pantomime of her own.

By chance, at the Royal School in the Windsor Home Park, where the children of workers on the Royal estates are educated, was the very man to help, the headmaster, Mr. Hubert Tannar, whose great hobby was amateur theatricals. With his aid, a script was written, a cast chosen, and *Cinderella*, the first of the Royal pantomimes, was under way. Princess Elizabeth put her energies whole-heartedly into the job as she has the habit of doing with everything she tackles, and "script conferences", rehearsals, dance and song "try-outs" began to occupy more and more of the out-of-study hours of both Princesses, for Princess Margaret, who has both shrewd powers of observation and a keen wit of her own, took her full share in all these activities, particularly in the script writing. Cinderella was a well-enough worn theme, but, in the true tradition of pantomime, the Princesses decided that anything and everything might be dragged into the story, provided it made for laughter. Family jokes with hidden allusions, references to the latest war developments, sly friendly quips about members of the Household, all went into the "book", which no one outside the cast was allowed to know anything about in advance. And whenever anyone who might be considered to know about theatrical matters arrived at the Castle, Princess Elizabeth made a point of asking their advice on some of her problems. Arthur Askey, George Formby, and Miss Florence Desmond were some of the Princess's "consultants" in this respect.

Like other wartime producers, the Princess and her companions had to face the twin problems of scenery and dresses. Members of the Castle staff, delighted to help, set to and stitched clothes and costumes from all sorts of scrap material, while the superintendent of the Castle, Mr. Stanley Williams, and his staff took on the task of making and painting backcloths, scenery, and various property effects. Most of the casting problems were comparatively easy. Princess Elizabeth would be Prince Charming, Princess Margaret, Cinderella, the schoolmaster enthusiast, the senior comedian, while other parts could go to the Princess's friends, with the Royal School children to provide the chorus. But there remained the problem of a young comedian to play opposite the Princesses, and here the story of the Royal pantomimes takes on a more fairy-tale quality than ever, for it was a young office-boy in the Supply Department of the Castle who was selected by the Princess for this part. Cyril Woods, then aged fifteen, had been such a success in the first Christmas concert, that he was the obvious choice, and so well did he acquit himself that in each of the three succeeding pantomimes, he remained the star comedian, playing Widow Twankey to Princess Elizabeth's Aladdin, and Old Mother Hubbard to her Lady Christina. Details of the first pantomimes were kept semi-secret, but later, when the King allowed reports to appear mentioning Cyril Woods, and telling the story of the Princess and the office boy, theatrical and film agents began to be interested in him. Unmoved by all this publicity and fuss, the level-headed young man, with a natural gift for mimicry that many professionals would envy, went back each year to his office work as a junior, addressing quite minor members of the staff as "Sir" the day after he had been acting and joking with the two Princesses. It was a situation in which Barrie —Princess Margaret's long-established favourite author—would have taken delight, a situation which could occur nowhere else in the world save at the Court of the King of England.

To-day, when the last of the pantomimes has been played, Woods is still at work in an office as a junior, in the Accountants Department at Buckingham Palace. Sometimes as he checks bills and goes about his daily routine task, he must think back to those amazing days when the King's two daughters stood back to give him the centre of the stage . . .

For Princess Elizabeth and Princess Margaret, each of the pantomimes was a personal triumph. The Royal sisters sing and dance together extremely well; indeed, singing duets to the King and Queen is a favourite enjoyment of theirs, but there is a considerable difference between that and appearing on a stage, and it was a fully equipped, large stage, with footlights, spotlights, curtains, changing scenery and other effects on which the Princesses played their parts to an audience including, besides the King and Queen and other members of their family, scores of strangers, and, at one performance each

THE FAIRY TALE OF WINDSOR

year, detachments of Guardsmen from Windsor Barracks who came by special invitation from Princess Elizabeth. It was not, therefore, the easiest of audiences, but the Princesses, especially Princess Margaret, played with a lack of self-consciousness that was delightful to watch, throwing themselves completely into their parts. To hear them in the last of their pantomimes, *Old Mother Red Riding Boots*, a happy mixture of half a dozen traditional pantomime stories, sing the old French nursery rhyme, "Sur le Pont d'Avignon" in "The Glade of the Crystal Stream" was an unforgettable experience. First they sang it in the original manner as a nursery rhyme, then in modern "swing" time, in which guise "Sur le Pont" is one of Princess Elizabeth's favourite dance tunes. They sang, in that same pantomime, "Come into the Garden, Maud", and here, too, all was not quite as the original composer intended, for "Lady Christina Sherwood" (Princess Elizabeth) and "The Hon. Lucy Fairfax" (Princess Margaret) sang Tennyson's love poem in broad Cockney accents which would have made the refined Poet Laureate squirm, but which the 1944 audience enjoyed to the full—none more than the King, who laughed till the tears really did start in his eyes.

At all the pantomimes, the King was one of the most enthusiastic onlookers, attending the dress rehearsals and each of the two or three performances to which they were limited.

The simple, good-natured, straightforward humour made a direct appeal to him, and from nowhere in the crowded "house" came louder laughs than from the front row

"Prince Charming" and "Cinderella" at rehearsal.

where the King and Queen sat side by side. Playing Aladdin, Princess Elizabeth, who shares with her father a respect for the traditional and proper way of doing things, made her entrance by popping out of a laundry basket, as Aladdins have been wont to do for many a decade: and when, a little later, "Aladdin" remarked to "his" friends, "I don't know *what* they've been doing up at the Castle lately, they have so much washing every week", the King thoroughly enjoyed the joke, all the more because at that time soap and labour shortages made the Castle laundry much less than in peace time. Another home allusion which brought gusts of laughter from the King and Queen came in the same show, when Aladdin and Princess Roxana (Princess Margaret) discussed the "Coronation paintings" of the "Emperor and Empress" by "Sir Kerald Jelly" who, explained Princess Roxana to Aladdin, was finding great difficulty in getting the likeness of his sitters exactly as he wanted—a reference to the painstaking care with which Sir Gerald Kelly, R.A., was even then, in 1943, completing his State paintings of the King and Queen in their Coronation robes of 1937.

Popular tunes of the moment are always sung at Christmas pantomimes: and Princess Elizabeth followed ritual in this as well, sometimes altering the words to more appropriate phrasing. "In my Arms", "It's Foolish, but it's Fun", "Swinging on a Star", "Red, White and Blue Christmas" and other numbers of a similar kind figured in the programmes.

Ballet dancing has been an interest of Princess Elizabeth's since her very early years, when she had her first dancing lessons at 145, Piccadilly, and pas-de-deux by her and her sister were a feature of each of the shows. Both Princesses dance elegantly and gracefully, Princess Elizabeth particularly being an excellent tap dancer. For their last pantomime, the Princesses decided on a more ambitious dance programme than before. This time, they had a whole corps de ballet, eleven in number, trained and produced by Madame Vacani, the Princesses' own instructress, in a delightful ballet of the seaside in the 'nineties, with Princess Elizabeth at her most charming in a becoming long-skirted Victorian dress of pink, and a small brimmed straw hat, dancing a waltz with a "beau" in gay blazer and white flannels. Princess Margaret appeared as a schoolgirl of the period, and the other dancers were Misses Louise Cockcraft, Anne Crichton, Mary Morshead, Phoebe Morshead, Joan Parker, Dawn Simpson, Anne Verney, Carola Verney, and Karla Whetherall.

For this pantomime, *Old Mother Red Riding Boots*, Princess Elizabeth called in other professional advice as well. Mr. Vincent Korda and Mr. F. Bellan made scenery and effects for the show in a film studio, which resulted in a pleasant Christmas surprise for the Princesses, when Mr. Korda took over to Windsor a complete working model of their stage set, and asked them to accept it as a souvenir. She ordered costumes from a famous theatrical firm, wigs from another, and persuaded Mr. R. H. Wood, the B.B.C. sound engineer who supervises the King's broadcasts, to arrange for sound reproduction.

Historians of the future may find themselves baffled when they come upon evidence of another delightful touch inspired by the Princess for this occasion. All the pantomimes took place in the famous Waterloo Chamber of Windsor Castle, a lofty, well-proportioned room, within whose walls successive sovereigns have received each year, on June 18, anniversary of the battle, the silken Union Jack which forms the rent paid by the Iron Duke and his successors for the Wellington estates of Strathsfieldspey, and where, on

THE FAIRY TALE OF WINDSOR

Waterloo Night, it has been the custom to hold a state banquet in commemoration of the victory, with a hundred and fifty guests sitting at one huge mahogany table.

This room was built early in the nineteenth century on what had been an open court-yard, and the lofty walls of the surrounding buildings made a lantern light necessary, and ruled out windows. Its windowless walls are panelled with portraits of famous men of Napoleonic days, leaders of the Allied Powers who were victorious in 1814. King George III and King George IV, both in Garter robes, the first Duke of Wellington, Field Marshal von Blucher, the Emperor Alexander I of Russia, the Emperor Francis I of Austria, and King Frederick William III of Prussia, Prince Metternich, with generals, Cabinet ministers and plenipotentiaries, painted by Sir Thomas Lawrence, the President of the Royal Academy, by order of the Prince Regent, look down from the high walls. To preserve these paintings from possible bomb damage, they were removed with other Royal art treasures at the beginning of the war to a place of safety, and the high walls were left bare, with only the empty gilt frames to mark the vacant places, with the name of each portrait and its painter inscribed underneath.

Looking at these ugly empty spaces one day as she was making preliminary arrangements for the *Old Mother Red Riding Boots* pantomime, Princess Elizabeth had an idea. Why should they not be filled, temporarily at any rate, with paintings appropriate to the pantomime?

Pantomime Finale: the Princess has natural grace of movement, which blends with her tableau.

The Queen looks admiringly at her daughter as "Principal Boy", with Princess Margaret in her ball-dress as Cinderella.

A few weeks later, from the ornate frames that had housed the effigies of the men who beat Napoleon, a new and startling series of faces looked out, Aladdin rubbing his magic lamp, Mother Goose, her head apprehensively cocked, Cinderella in her glass slippers, and other familiar figures from the fairy land of make-believe. They had been painted by Mr. Claude Whatham, assisted by students from the Wycombe Technical Institute, in gay colours with a touch of fantasy that was exactly right. The Princess's idea was a great success. The pantomime figures on the walls added the needed background that had been missing before —though no one else had noticed it—to complete the transformation of the state room into a theatre. When the opening show of the pantomime came, everyone was loud in praise of the new scheme of decorations, and all was well.

That was in December 1944. Six months later, with the war in Europe over, when the Royal paintings began to return to Windsor Castle from their safe hiding place, among them Lawrence's studies of George III, George IV, their brother monarchs and their generals, the question came, what was to be done with the pantomime paintings in their frames. The King ruled that they should stay where they were. Perhaps his sense of humour was aroused at the thought of how shocked the proud Prussian feelings of Frederick William III would be on finding himself sharing a frame with Aladdin: and to-day, unguessed at by sightseers visiting the Castle, behind the solemn, formal paintings of the men who conquered at Waterloo and rewrote the history of Europe, are hidden the happy smiling figures of childhood's dreams. . . .

Some ungenerous-minded people seemed to find it contrary to their peculiar conceptions of what is proper and fitting for a King's daughter that Princess Elizabeth and her sister should be allowed to appear on the stage, even in the setting of their own home. Such false ideas of the necessity for cottonwool wrapping round the whole lives of Royalty have never found favour with the King and Queen. If Princess Elizabeth enjoyed the harmless amusement, they saw, of course, no reason to interfere; instead, they encouraged her and Princess Margaret in every way, believing that the active work of creating and producing the shows, as well as the many contacts they brought about, could be of nothing but benefit to their daughters.

The King became, as any father would, justly proud of his daughters' success: for it emphatically was a success that the Princesses scored each year. They danced and sang and mimed with such zest, such good stage sense, such excellence of rhythm and tune and time that their show, transferred to the West End as a children's performance, would easily have held its own. Each performance was singularly free from the wrong entries, the forgotten lines, the missed cues that usually mar amateur efforts of the kind. Princess Elizabeth saw to that. Setting herself the highest of standards, tireless in practice and rehearsal, she asked for—and obtained—equal enthusiasm from the rest of the cast, and no one watching the rehearsals could be left in doubt for long of her observant eye and powers of control. On the stage or off, Princess Elizabeth seemed to see everything that was going on. Was there a false step by one of the chorus, a fluffed line by a minor character, a piece of scenery wrongly placed, she was the first to notice and have it put right. That characteristic painstaking attention to detail by the Princess was one of the two secrets of the pantomime's success. The other was that everyone in the show, from the principal players to the scene shifters—and certainly the orchestra of the Royal Horse Guards who provided the music—thoroughly enjoyed being in it. Each year, after the last performance, the Princess gave a Christmas tea party to the whole cast, making a little speech of thanks to them for their co-operation and help. And there was equal, if unexpressed, gratitude to her on the part of them all for giving them the opportunity for so much fun.

It is probably from Queen Victoria, who was, in her younger days, much addicted to the theatre, frequently "commanding" famous actors and actresses to appear before her at Windsor, that the Princesses inherit their love of the stage. But the Royal family tradition of acting goes back a long way further than that. The three children of Charles I —the brothers, who became Charles II and James II, and the daughter, Princess Henrietta Maria—often acted in plays at the Palace of Whitehall to an audience of their father's courtiers and Ministers, and, later, King George III used to take part with other members of the Royal family in plays and presentations at Leicester House, coached by the famous actor Quin, and afterwards by Mrs. Siddons.

After *Old Mother Red Riding Boots*, however, there were to be no more Royal pantomimes. Princess Elizabeth was nearly nineteen when she made her appearance as "Lady Christina Sherwood" in that pantomime, and Princess Margaret, too, appeared as a girl, the "Hon. Lucinda Fairfax", with no principal boy in the cast. As pantomimes without principal boys are both difficult to devise and distinctly out of tradition, Princess Elizabeth decided, albeit with considerable reluctance, that her days as a pantomime star must come to an end—and the "Royal Company" dissolved. In any case, with the growing pressure of public duties, there would be little time in the future for the long hours of preparation, the talks and conferences, the script writing, the rehearsals, the hard work of production, which brought her as much enjoyment as the finished performances themselves. For the Princess, it was the end of an experience of great happiness and fun, one which she will remember all the days of her life.

Prince Philip, the Duke of Edinburgh, it should be recorded, never took part in any of the Royal pantomimes. But he saw his future wife act in one of them, *Aladdin*, when he was staying at Windsor Castle on a Christmas leave in 1943.

CHAPTER SEVEN

Princess in Khaki

HALF a dozen lines of an official announcement issued from Buckingham Palace just over a month before her nineteenth birthday revealed the surprising news that Princess Elizabeth had joined the Auxiliary Territorial Service, and was taking a driving course.

The news was surprising because, twelve months before, the nation had been given clearly to understand that for the Princess, entry into any of the three women's services, or any other form of normal war service, was out of the question, since the claims of her training as heiress to the throne must come first. In the year that had passed, the public, almost without exception, had come to accept this decision as wise and right. Now, apparently, there was a complete reversal of Royal policy. The terms of the Palace announcement did nothing to clear up the mystery. It ran simply in these words:—"The King has granted to Her Royal Highness the Princess Elizabeth a commission with the honorary rank of second subaltern in the Auxiliary Territorial Service. Her Royal Highness is at present undergoing a course at a driving training centre in the south of England." The pith of the matter was in a semi-official adjunct to the announcement, which stated that this step had been taken "at the Princess's own request".

Behind those few words lies a revealing story of the strength of Princess Elizabeth's character, a story of how a Royal girl's determination caused a decision, made with Cabinet approval, to be reversed.

One by one, as war went on, she had seen her girl friends following their fathers and brothers—and in some cases their mothers as well—into the Services, joining one or other of the three women's services. When they came on leave, she heard from them the stories of new interests, new adventures, new companionships that homecoming warriors have told ever since the world was young, adventures and interests that she herself could never share, because, as she well knew, it had been decided that the necessity for her training for public life and future queenship to go on without interruption outweighed all other considerations, was of greater importance than any other form of service to the nation which she could possibly undertake.

As a subject of His Majesty, even though she happened to be the King's elder daughter, the Princess came under the provisions of the National Service Act, and had, indeed, registered for service as a junior at the age of sixteen. But hers was obviously a special case, requiring the personal consideration and attention of the Minister of Labour and National Service, Mr. Ernest Bevin, himself, and, doubtless, that of his colleagues in Mr. Churchill's Cabinet. After long and careful consideration, with the sanction of the King, and, therefore, the implicit approval of the War Cabinet, an official statement was issued from Buckingham Palace, on the eve of the Princess's eighteenth birthday, setting forth the position, and explaining why it had been decided that she should neither join one of

In working dungarees, the Heiress Presumptive changes a wheel:
her A.T.S. driving course was very thorough.

the women's services, nor work at a munitions factory, as nearly all other girls of eighteen were doing. Only people with the most prejudiced of minds could find fault with this eminently reasonable ruling, which gained general approval throughout the country and the Empire.

But there was one person at least who did not take a good view of it at all; and that was Princess Elizabeth. She could not, of course, make her dissentient voice heard in public: but in private, a good deal must have been going on behind the scenes in the way of argument and persuasion, until, a year later, the Princess scored a real personal triumph by gaining from her father a commission in the A.T.S. Though but few people realised it at the time, the announcement of her appointment was a direct pointer to a very important feature in the make-up of the heiress to the throne, her decided, determined character, and her no small measure of ability to get her own way in the face of strong opposition. It showed, too, that the Princess has the same gift of Royal intuition as her father, that instinctive understanding of what is the right thing to do, sometimes even against official advice, that is one of the corner stones of the British monarchy's strength.

Her decision was widely popular, and the way in which she carried it out more popular still, for the King, giving his consent to the appointment, had stipulated that his daughter

H

In dungarees, before beginning her morning's instruction at the A.T.S.
Motor Training Centre. The Princess much enjoyed her days with the
girls in khaki.
Photograph: Crown Copyright Reserved.

*Honorary Second Subaltern H.R.H. The Princess Elizabeth :
a studio portrait in khaki.*

should be treated in exactly the same way as any other officer trainee at the training centre. She was to receive no special privileges because of her personal rank, any more than the King himself did when he served in the Royal Navy and the Royal Air Force. From the first day she arrived at the private house, lying just off the main road into Camberley, which was the headquarters of No. 1 Mechanical Transport Training Centre of the A.T.S., Princess Elizabeth herself insisted that these orders should be strictly interpreted, and soon made it clear that she would dislike any attempt to make things easier for her because she was of Royal birth. In this connection, one point had to be given special consideration. Besides the normal wartime security silence, it was necessary to take extra precautions to guard the Princess's privacy, if gaping crowds were to be avoided. Sightseers following her every movement as she worked, or driving behind her when she was out under instruction, would have completely defeated the whole plan for her training, so, a few days before she was due to join the course, the commandant of the centre, a woman of wide experience, called all her officers together, told them of the honour that had been done their centre, and pointed out the imperative need for secrecy about the Princess's coming among them. The officers told the other ranks that evening, not even putting them on their honour, but leaving it to their own good sense and judgement not to talk. These steps resulted in a proof that a thousand girls *can* keep a secret, for even in the neighbouring town of Camberley a mile or so away, no one knew or even suspected the Princess was in camp until after the official announcement.

Not only the thousand lucky ones whose period at No. 1 Training Centre coincided with the Princess's stay, but girls in the A.T.S. all over the country were naturally delighted when they heard that the King's daughter had chosen their service in preference to the other two. The A.T.S. was, dare it be suggested, the third, rather than the first, choice of most fashionable young women on enrolling. The Princess had received her pre-entry training as a Sea Ranger, which clearly marked her out as a future candidate for the W.R.N.S., and she certainly enjoyed that advantage which was almost a *sine qua non* for the women's branch of the senior service, a father who was a naval officer. Perhaps the influence of her aunt, the Princess Royal, who devoted her energies so wholeheartedly throughout the war to the work of the A.T.S., of which she is Controller Commandant, is not without its bearing in this connection, or perhaps the Princess, wishing to make entirely new contacts, preferred to seek new experience in a service whose ways and methods were completely novel to her.

Whatever was the cause, it was the A.T.S. which the Princess chose, to the high and undisguised delight of all the other girls in khaki throughout the length and breadth of the land, and it is on record that the angle of tilt of the A.T.S. noses was noticeably higher in the week or two following the announcement of her choice.

Once she had made her decision, the Princess carried it through purposefully and thoroughly. Up till then, it is doubtful whether the hands of the daughter of a reigning sovereign had ever been soiled with car oil and gear grease, but when the practical side of the instruction course involved dismantling and reassembling engines, re-timing valves, changing wheels on heavy lorries, and the rest of the more unpleasant tasks that are usually relegated to chauffeurs or garage mechanics, the Princess did not falter, or shirk at the thought of grimy hands. On the contrary, she was intensely proud of the signs of mechanical toil on her hands, which she showed to her friends with great glee. She set to

Changing plugs and other "under the bonnet" jobs came the Princess's way at the A.T.S. Motoring School.

with a will, and was immensely pleased when, after the first day or two of constraint had passed, the other girls—who, incidentally, called her at her own request simply "Princess" and not "Your Royal Highness", if they were of equal or higher rank, and plain "Ma'am" as they did any other officer in the case of lower ranks—accepted and treated her as one of themselves. It was a test, and a test of a very special kind, for the Princess. She passed that exceptionally difficult test in human relationships with as full, if not fuller, marks as she did the driving and theory tests that ended her course.

The Princess enjoyed everything about her new life, and quickly made friends with a number of her fellow pupils. She took the altered conditions of life in her stride, settling down on the easiest of terms with her senior officers, her equals, and her subordinates alike. But if the Princess could take it all calmly, not all the rest of the A.T.S. could follow her example, as instance the case of one veteran girl-driver, herself an ex-pupil of No. 1 M.T. Centre, who had to drive a very senior A.T.S. officer down on a visit of inspection to see how the Royal pupil was progressing.

Just as she was backing her car into position after dropping her passenger, the A.T.S. driver saw Princess Elizabeth run down the steps of the officers' mess and get into the driving seat of an Army car, exactly similar to the one she was driving. It was the first time the A.T.S. girl had ever seen the Princess, and that, coupled with the thought that the King's daughter was doing the same job as she was, proved too much for her. Forgetting in her curiosity and excitement one of the chief rules she had learned at the Centre, she took her eyes off where she was going to look at the Princess. Her car crashed into a marking post, knocking it sideways. Princess Elizabeth, who misses very little of what goes on around her, saw the incident and smiled. By good fortune for the driver, no one else had seen what happened, and later she drove off with her officer-passenger without the reprimand she knew she had earned. But the leaning post was left leaning for some days, as an example to other drivers to attend to the job in hand no matter who might be passing.

The Princess's working hours were the same as for the rest of the "cadre", from 10 a.m. to 5 p.m. Each day ended with a routine cleaning of the vehicle she had been using, a check up on the oil, battery and radiator levels, and an engine test for smooth running. When she began instruction, she was a complete novice, her driving experience confined entirely to being a passenger in the Royal limousines and an occasional ride in her father's private car. Some of her fellow students were novices, too, but the majority were already qualified drivers, taking an N.C.O.'s refresher course. The Princess's two companions in her "syndicate" were sergeants, one with a husband fighting in the artillery in Italy.

The Army does not believe that the easiest way is always the best, and the first vehicle Princess Elizabeth had to handle was a fifteen hundredweight Army truck on blocks. When she had mastered the controls sufficiently, she went out on the roads, in trucks, six-cylinder motor ambulances, and staff cars, to gain experience of all types, driving at night in the appalling black-out conditions, as well as on the traffic-thronged roads by day. Besides all this she had to learn the whole theory of the "Otto cycle", the working of differentials and universal joints, gear-boxes and clutches, all the arcana of the internal combustion engine and its accessories which most motorists are well content to leave as mysteries as long as the car continues to go. She studied map reading, the highway code, and similar subjects. When the instructress would give the class a map reference to locate, it was open to any girl to put her hand up first—but only rarely was the Princess beaten. She has a naturally quick intelligence, which she was using to such good purpose that the Commandant declared "All of us here have found the Princess extremely quick to learn. When she came, she had never driven a car of any kind, and she has learned to drive much more quickly than the average run of girls," adding that the Princess had turned into an "excellent and very considerate driver. She is not rash, and drives with thought for others on the road." To this, the Princess's own instructress, Miss V. Wellesley, who served in the 1914–18 war as a motor-cycle dispatch rider in the W.A.A.C., added another tribute: "The Princess drives with consideration and care for her car."

Other A.T.S. girls took a tremendous interest in the Princess's progress. When the King and Queen were visiting a Manchester Service Club, one of them, a sergeant-driver, plucked up courage to ask the Queen about her.

With some trepidation, the girl waited, thinking perhaps she had presumed too much. But the Queen smiled with real pleasure, and told her "Princess Elizabeth is enjoying being in the A.T.S. very much. She is learning to drive a lorry just now, and she seems to spend most of her time diving underneath it!"—a sidelight on Royal activities that quickly went the rounds of the whole A.T.S.

No favouritism was the rule all through the Princess's course, yet a most careful check of her service log showed she had finished in a shorter time than any other girl in her class, passing out as a fully qualified and competent driver on Saturday, April 14, 1945. She had learned to change wheels, to adjust carburettors, to grind in valves, to decarbonise an engine, to re-time it, and to carry out most kinds of running repairs, pitting her brain for the first time in fair, equal and open competition with other girls—and she passed the test with flying colours. Two years later, the Princess took on temporary duty as a civilian instructor and taught Princess Margaret to drive.

Out on the roads, the same rule of "no favouritism" applied. "Hon. Second Subaltern the Princess Elizabeth", whose Army number was 230873, had to take her chance with the rest of the road-users, Service and civilian. The former motor-cycle dispatch rider, who had braved all sorts of perils in France driving behind the British lines in 1914–18, accompanied her on all her road lessons.

Well-used to the vagaries of inexperienced drivers, and inured to being driven along the roads round and about on No. 1 M.T. Centre, in heavy Army lorries by young women who had only just passed their road tests, she can have had no nerves at all. But even such a perfectly controlled passenger may well have felt certain qualms when the King's daughter insisted, as she did, on going out on the roads like the other girls and driving through the traffic on Bank Holiday Monday, with every available private car on the road to Ascot Races. Clad in her khaki battle dress, the Princess drove calmly through the tangle of civilian and military traffic, handling the camouflaged Army car as easily and confidently as if she had been driving her pony-cart in the secluded empty avenues

In A.T.S. uniform the Princess inspects girl officer-cadets at the Imperial Service College.

of Windsor Great Park. No one, outside the officers and staff at the Training Centre, knew that she was on the road, and many a Berkshire constable, holding up the workaday car with its obvious tyro driver and her instructor, to let the "priority" race traffic pass, might well have dropped his controlling arm in surprise had he recognised Princess Elizabeth at the wheel. But no one did recognise her. She drove the car back to the Centre without incident, garaged and cleaned it, and was able to tell the King and Queen an amusing tale of her day of Haroun-al-Raschid adventures.

At that time, I have been told, the conversation at the Royal dinner table at Windsor Castle, whenever Princess Elizabeth was able to join her parents there, tended to centre round sparking plugs, rotor arms, dynamos, crankshafts and so on, a feature which must have been a source of considerable amusement to the King, who has himself been interested in things mechanical to such an extent that more than once in his days as a young officer in the R.A.F. he was chipped for being too "engine-minded".

To the Princess, the greatest day of her whole stay with the A.T.S. was when the King and Queen came to inspect the Centre, and to see her at work. This was not her first experience of a Royal visit from the "other side", for a few days earlier, the Princess Royal had come to the Centre to see how her niece was progressing.

But when her mother and father came, it was the first time she had ever been on the "receiving end" of a visit by Their Majesties. Princess Margaret, who had heard a great deal from her sister about her experiences at the Centre, came with the King and Queen, and looked round expectantly for her sister as she got out of the King's car. But Princess Elizabeth was nowhere to be seen among the group of khaki-clad A.T.S. officers receiving the Royal party. With a ramrod-stiff woman sergeant-major walking in front, the King and Queen went slowly round the Centre inspecting the class rooms, the workshops and the rest of the Centre. Still there was no sign of the Princess. Then, in one workshop, there was a little group of girls in overalls, leaning over the engine of a camouflaged lorry. One of them looked up with a grin, and Princess Margaret recognised her sister. The Princess was just carrying on her ordinary day's work while her father, mother and sister made their inspection. Her hands were thick with oil, her overall stained with grease, as she stood chatting to her family for a few moments. Then the Royal party moved on, leaving the Princess behind. Some time later, as they made their way back, the King and Queen found Princess Elizabeth and her comrades still busy on the lorry. "Haven't you got it mended yet?" the King asked his daughter. The Princess smiled and went on with the job.

At tea-time, the Princess reverted for a brief while to Royal status, and joined the King and Queen and Princess Margaret with the senior officers in the mess.

As the big Royal limousine, with its familiar maroon and red body, its gilt radiator mascot of Britannia bright and gleaming, its chassis bare, as always, of number plates, for the King need pay no road tax to travel in whatsoever manner he wishes on what is still, legally, the King's Highway, drove slowly away, Princess Elizabeth stood in the gravel drive outside the mess, waving good-bye to her parents. She gazed for some moments at the receding car, then turned to the other A.T.S. girls with a smile that seemed to express a faint hope that the miraculous might happen, the Royal car *might* break down on the way home, and Hawes, the King's chauffeur, *might* have to call her to the rescue, to pick up her father and mother and drive them home. Alas for the

*At the wheel: the Princess ready to take an
ambulance on the road.*

Princess-driver's hopes! The King's car proceeded uneventfully on its way and reached Windsor Castle, as usual, without incident.

The Princess and her sister officers went into the mess again to talk over the events of the day. Naturally, the Royal visit was the chief topic of conversation. Various officers made various comments. Then came the turn of the Princess who had taken her full part in the tidying up and cleaning processes that had occupied so much time during the past two days. "I'd no idea before how much preparation has to be made in advance of a Royal visit," she said. "Next time I go anywhere, on an official occasion, I'll know something about what has been done beforehand!"

That remark by the Princess shows not only the value of the training she herself had selected, but also, surely, her ability to profit from it. It was an observation that unconsciously, but none the less exactly, interprets the spirit of our constitutional monarchy, the kind of remark which you cannot, by the wildest stretch of imagination, conceive of a dictator, or a dictator's "heir" making in any circumstances at all.

After the excitement of the Royal visit had died down, the Princess and her fellow students went quietly on with their studies theoretical and practical, until the last day of the course came. Each and all of them had driven staff cars, light trucks, ambulances and heavy Army lorries round the Aldershot roads. Each and all of them—the Princess along with the rest—had heard the jesting "encouragements" that other (male) military drivers were apt to utter on seeing an Army car bearing the letter "L" and driven by a girl in khaki battledress. Each and all of them felt confident enough until it came to the examination day, when there was little to choose between them in the way of nerves as they faced their final tests. But all passed with varying degrees of success, leaving one last trial, not included in the formal War Office schedule for the course, to be faced. As a kind of reward for good behaviour, and at the same time, as a practical test under the most gruelling conditions, it had become customary at the Centre for successful candidates to finish off with a drive up to London, accompanied of course by an instructress, to gain experience of driving in traffic at its thickest.

Princess Elizabeth, who had shared all the other tests, all the instruction, all the discomforts and all the fun of the course with the other girls wanted to share in this, too. The woman commandant of the Centre, a lady of great experience and wisdom, was in full support of the Princess's wish. Not to allow her to drive to London like all the rest would, she felt, possibly give her Royal pupil something of a feeling of inferiority and restriction, which was precisely what the whole scheme of the training was designed to avoid. But other weighty considerations were involved. If the heiress to the Throne were to become, albeit through no fault of her own, involved in a serious road accident, as well might happen to any driver, however experienced, what would be the position of the A.T.S. authorities who had given permission for the drive? What would the Home Secretary, charged with the responsibility for the safety of the Royal family, have to say? And what about the police? If they were informed, they would probably insist on providing a motor-cycle escort or a pilot car, either of which would ruin the whole purpose of the drive. On the other hand, not to let the police authorities know of the Princess's movements might involve serious consequences. After much weighing of the arguments for and against, it was decided that the possible disadvantages and dangers overbalanced the good points, so the scheme was abandoned, unless higher authorities ruled otherwise.

The next act in this little Royal comedy had for its setting the smooth dull red gravel forecourt of Buckingham Palace, behind the black and gold railings through which London crowds love to peer at the changing of the Guard. Then, they still showed ugly gaps, boarded with wood planking, where Hitler's bombs had fallen on the King of England's home. It was the evening of a party given by the King and Queen for Dominion visitors to London. Car after car, black civilian saloons, khaki military runabouts, cars with the badges of France and Poland and our other allies swept through the Palace gates, with the police holding up the constant stream of traffic from the Mall and Constitution Hill to let them enter and deposit their occupants at the Grand Entrance on the far side of the inner quadrangle. Most guests had already arrived when yet another small closed car, wearing military camouflage and War Office markings, drove round the Victoria Memorial in obedience to the one-way traffic rule, and turned left-handed into the Palace gates. It takes a very great deal to astonish a member of the Metropolitan Police Force, but the constable who held up the traffic for that particular car was a very surprised man indeed as he recognised the driver, and hurriedly raised his hand to his helmet in salute. It was Princess Elizabeth, her face radiating satisfaction as, for the very first time, she drove a car through the gates of her father's Palace. At her side sat her faithful instructress.

When the Princess heard that she was to attend the party, it seemed a golden opportunity. After all, she *had* to get from Camberley to London by car, so why not drive herself? And it would be very pleasant to invite Miss Wellesley to the Palace, in which case she could come up to town with the Princess just as she did with other newly-passed drivers. Few of the people who met her at the party had any inkling of what it was that prompted the even more than usually high spirits in which they found the Princess that evening, and even the policeman, still meditating, as he stood on duty at the gates, on what surprising things may happen in modern wartime London, could not guess all that lay behind the Princess's sparkling eyes, smiles and satisfaction.

Not content with merely driving through the thick traffic of homeward-bound London in the early evening at the time when lighting conditions are at their worst from the driver's point of view, the Princess had come by a roundabout route, deliberately chosen to include as many of the most-used traffic roads as possible. She had driven along Oxford Street, down Regent Street, and not once but twice round Piccadilly Circus, all, of course, without police escort or any of the usual precautions of closed roads, held-up traffic and switched-off traffic lights which are the normal accompaniments of Royal drives, when a fully trained and widely experienced chauffeur has charge of the Royal car. Instead, the Princess had taken her chance, just as she wanted to, in the ordinary whirl of buses, taxis, private cars and hurrying pedestrians, obeying the light signals, the thirty miles an hour speed limit, and all the other rules of the road just like any other motorist. It was an experience that few members of the Royal family, and certainly no young Princess of nineteen, had ever enjoyed before. Enjoyed is the exact word, for Princess Elizabeth enjoyed every moment of it. She drove back, later, to Camberley, but that was the end, for the time being, at any rate, of her London driving experience. Highly-placed police officials, even the Home Secretary, Mr. Herbert Morrison himself, breathed much more easily when they heard that the determined young Royal driver had accomplished her wish in perfect safety. But repetitions of the risk were not to be thought of, a decision which the Princess sensibly and readily accepted when it was made known to her.

That story, typical of Princess Elizabeth as she is to-day, is worth telling at some length, because it illustrates several important aspects of her character, her determination to overcome obstacles in her way, her thoroughness in carrying through to its proper end any undertaking to which she has put her hand, and her innate good-sense and strength of mind in realising when and where her private inclinations and desires, however compelling, must perforce give way to her public duties and responsibilities. The dual strength of character that episode reveals augurs excellently for the future, when the weight of duty and responsibility becomes heavier and more pressing, when the clash between private wishes and Royal duties may be of more serious import. It indicates, too, in no uncertain fashion, the way the Princess's mind reacts in such circumstances. If it is practicable to do what she wishes, if it is nothing but red-tape and conventional tradition (think what Queen Victoria would have had to say on the subject of one of her sons, let alone a daughter, driving a dog-cart or even a four-in-hand through the Palace gates!) that stand in the way, she will press until she gains her point. But when there are sound and serious reasons why she should refrain from some course of action, she is always ready to put duty foremost.

Many young women out of uniform to-day, recalling perhaps only the jollier parts of their Service days, are apt to look back on the time they spent in the W.R.N.S., the A.T.S. or the W.A.A.F., as the best time of their lives. Princess Elizabeth was not allowed to see enough of Service life to be able to share or to disagree with that view, but she certainly did enjoy all the brief time she spent with the A.T.S. driving unit. At the Centre, amid a crowd of girls drawn haphazardly from all over the country, from all ranks and all classes, she had for the first, and possibly for the only time in her life, an opportunity of meeting other girls of her own age, but with widely different backgrounds and outlooks, on almost level terms. To some extent, it afforded her the kind of experience which her father and her grandfather before him had both undergone in the Royal Navy with such profit to them in after-years, experience which, outside wartime conditions, would have been most difficult, if not impossible, to arrange for her without complete artificiality. Girls at the training centre were divided, for convenience in instruction, into "working parties" of threes, or "syndicates" as they were known, and the two girls who were to be the Princess's closest companions were, it is true, selected with a certain amount of care. But that was as far as selection went. No girls were drafted specially to the Centre, nor were any excluded on account of birth or position because the Princess would be their fellow student. Girls due for a driving course in that area at that time were automatically posted to the Centre, and served with their future Queen. Others who came later or were in a different military zone missed the chance.

The selfsame reasons of State which prompted the original decision that the Princess should not join the Services or go into a factory made it clearly impossible for her to continue full-time duty with the A.T.S. Other and more important matters claimed her attention, for the time was now drawing near when she must begin to take her active part in public life. The nation at large wanted to see the Heiress Presumptive, and this clearly-voiced call could not be answered by time spent, however profitably, segregated in a unit of any of the Services. So, after she had completed her driving course, Princess Elizabeth gradually withdrew from active participation in the life of the A.T.S., though the interests of the girls in khaki of whom she had herself been one remained from then onwards very close to her.

She was "granted the honorary rank of junior commander", in the severely formal language of the London Gazette used to indicate that there can be no "promotion" in honorary rank, on July 26, 1945, and made her first public appearance wearing the insignia of her new rank appropriately enough at the Motor Transport Training Centre she had quitted not long before. This time, the Princess went, not as a junior officer of the A.T.S., but as a Royal visitor, and on the parade ground, which she knew so well,

she stood on a dais to receive the salute of her erstwhile comrades, after she had made a solemn, grave-faced inspection of their ranks. Then came an incident which delighted the Princess. Up to her marched the smartly-uniformed Regimental-Sergeant-Major with the same ramrod back which she had so often seen, the same staccato voice she had so often heard on morning parades, halted, saluted with Guards-like precision—and presented to the Royal ex-pupil a remembrance from officers and girls of the Centre of the days she had spent with them. It was a clock, made in the Centre's workshops, and decorated with models of all the vehicles the Princess had driven during her course. That clock to-day occupies a place of honour in the Princess's private apartments.

While she was on active duty with the A.T.S., Princess Elizabeth necessarily wore uniform all the time. The first sight the public had of her in khaki was at the last of the wartime "South Cup Finals" at Wembley, on April 8, 1945, to which she went with the

With military smartness, the Princess takes the salute at Slough.

123

King and Queen. She wore a greatcoat and soft-topped service cap, and onlookers noted both how smartly she wore her uniform, and how much more "grown-up" she seemed. A month or two beforehand, she had looked a mere girl: now she was a young woman.

Later, during the final months of the war in Europe, a good many people were baffled by newsreels and newspaper pictures of the Princess, which showed her sometimes in khaki uniform, sometimes, even on military occasions, in plain civilian attire. At parades of the Grenadier Guards which she attended as Colonel, she wore civilian attire to avoid the paradoxical situation of receiving, in the uniform of a junior officer, the salutes of senior officers of the Guards.

On other occasions of a formal nature, when she was appearing in public with the King, she wore, as she was, of course, fully entitled to do, her uniform. On VE Day, for example, it was in uniform that the Princess appeared on the balcony of Buckingham Palace with her father, mother and sister as the roars of the great crowds in the Mall swelled up in victorious greeting to the Sovereign and his family: and it was in khaki greatcoat and service cap that she laid her first wreath on the Cenotaph in Whitehall on the first Armistice Day of peace.

Another point about the Princess's uniform that caused some enquiries was the fact that she wore, from the very first day of joining the A.T.S., two medal ribbons on her tunic. Knowing that she could not possibly have gained any military awards in advance, yet certain that if she wore medal ribbons, she was undoubtedly possessed of whatever decorations they represented, a large section of the community without much knowledge of ribbons and their colours wondered what the solution of the little problem could be. The answer was quite simple. Both the Princess's ribbons were coloured red, white and blue, the first with a deep red ground, edged on either side with a narrow double band of dark blue enclosing a white band, the second with a ground of royal blue, edged on either side with a double band of white, enclosing a red band. The first medal was given her by her grandfather, King George V, when she was nine years old. It was the medal of his Silver Jubilee. The second is the Coronation medal she received two years later from her father. To them are now added the blue of the Order of the Garter, and the white of the Imperial Order of the Crown of India.

The theory and practice of the internal combustion engine, the Highway Code, and the other necessary subjects which A.T.S. driving personnel had to acquire, were not the limit of Princess Elizabeth's Service experience. She underwent an intensified course of training in A.T.S. law and general regulations, and a brief but comprehensive period of instruction in the drill and discipline of the "women's section" of the Army, which included several lectures by high ranking A.T.S. officers in London.

The Princess's service in the A.T.S. was the culmination of a long period of what has become known by the ugly name of "pre-service training" with its potential implications of future war. But war and national service in the armed forces were far from the thoughts of Princess Elizabeth, as they were from the thoughts of most of us in this country, eleven years ago, when, at the joint inspiration of her aunt, the Princess Royal, herself President of the Girl Guides' Association, and of "Crawfie", otherwise Miss Marion Crawford, her governess, she formed with a number of her young girl friends the Buckingham Palace Company of Girl Guides.

PRINCESS IN KHAKI

It was while she and her sister Princess Margaret were in Scotland with their parents, who were relaxing at Balmoral after the strenuous days of the Coronation, that the Princess first formed the idea of setting up a company of Guides from among her own friends. She had read much about Guide activities, and had heard even more from her aunt, from "Crawfie", and from the Queen, who was an enthusiastic Guide herself in her young days at Glamis Castle and St. Paul's Walden, her home in Hertfordshire. Now, she thought, the time had come for her to be a Guide herself. The Queen's permission was sought and most willingly given. When the Royal family returned to London, the Princess attended the first meeting she had ever called together, at which about a dozen of her friends and some younger girls who were Princess Margaret's playmates unanimously agreed to the formation of the new company. Officially, on the roll of the Girl Guides' Association, it was entered as the "7th Westminster Company", with its headquarters address given as "Buckingham Palace, S.W.1.". The Queen put a room in the Palace entirely at the disposal of the Guides, and there company business was transacted, Guide "law" studied, and preparations made for the passing of various proficiency tests and so on. Even at that early age—she was eleven when the company was formed—Princess Elizabeth showed signs of that thoroughness and application and refusal to take undue advantage of her rank that have remained among her chief characteristics till to-day.

She wanted, naturally enough, to be the leader of her patrol, but this was a distinction to be achieved only by merit, not to be bestowed by the fortune of Royal birth, so that

Youth honours its Royal representative: a girl cadet offers Princess Elizabeth a bouquet.

it was not until nearly two years after the formation of the company that the Princess became leader of the Kingfisher Patrol of Guides, which, together with the Leprechaun Section of the Brownies, to which Princess Margaret belonged, made up the "Seventh Westminsters", more generally known as the Buckingham Palace Company of Girl Guides.

An interesting pointer to the world-wide interest in the activities of the Princesses, and the unsuspected results their actions may have, is the fact that as a result of their signing the roll of Girl Guides and Brownies in London two trees were named after them at Kuala Lumpur, half-way across the world, in distant Malaya. Chinese, Indian, Malay and Eurasian girls enrolled in the local Guides were so delighted to hear that the King's daughters had joined their movement that they decided to plant two trees in their honour, and name them after them, at their Guide headquarters at Kuala Lumpur.

Both Princesses took their Guide training with intense seriousness, and devoted all the time they could spare to Guide work. When the Court moved to Sandringham for the long winter stays that were customary in peace time, the Princesses, separated from their fellow members, carried out practice "drills" on their own, marching and turning on the cement washdowns in front of the Royal garages, eager to gain their proficiency badges as soon as possible. Back at the Palace, regular weekly drills went on every Wednesday afternoon, with the "parade" on the wide Palace lawns in fine weather, indoors, if it were wet, in the big room on the second floor, once used as a schoolroom by the King and his brothers and sister, and now one of the suite of three rooms that form Princess Elizabeth's own apartments in the Palace. The Queen did all she could to encourage her daughters' new and absorbing interest. She gave the Company two flags, a Union Jack, and Company Colours of red and blue, for Christmas, and herself attended the dedication ceremony in the private chapel of the Palace.

As a Guide the Princess learned to tie knots, to make a bed neatly, to build and light a safe camp fire, how to treat cuts, bruises and sprains, to send and receive messages in morse and semaphore. It was in the blue tunic and pleated skirt of a Guide, with Princess Margaret at her side in Brownie outfit, that the Princess made her first public appearance in uniform, at a big march past of over one thousand Girl Guides, from all parts of the Empire, who attended a National Guides Service at St. George's Chapel, Windsor, in June 1938. Few, if any, of the watching crowds on that bright Sunday afternoon, can have dreamed that the Princess would one day be donning a more serious, purposeful uniform of khaki with her father's Empire at war! To emphasise the equality of treatment meted out in the Guides, neither of the King's daughters were allowed to attend the actual service in the chapel. Only first-class Guides, those who have passed advanced tests, were invited to the service, and, as neither Princess had this qualification, neither could go into the chapel.

In the early part of the war, the Princesses went on with their Guide training in Scotland, where they spent some months at Balmoral. Later, when their wartime home was set up at Windsor, the activities of the Buckingham Palace Company were transferred there. By this time, Princess Elizabeth had passed all her Guide tests, and early in 1943 she qualified as a Sea Ranger. The girls of the "Kingfisher Patrol" now became members of the "crew" of the *President III* as the Princess christened her "ship" after the famous R.N.R. training ship on the Thames. To show his appreciation, the King presented the Rangers with a ship's "whaler" and dinghies for their exclusive use on the lake at

Frogmore, which enabled the Princesses to get in a great deal of water-training and to learn the practical side of handling boats, side by side with the theoretical training in compass reading, navigation, and so on. The Rangers went for frequent river trips on the Thames, too, in one of the Home Guard motor launches.

In the Waterloo Chamber of Windsor Castle, which takes its name from the annual banquet formerly given to commemorate the great victory, the King gave permission for a complete replica of the bridge of a man o' war to be constructed for the Rangers' use, fitted with engine-room telegraphs, compass, voice pipes, lifebelts and other nautical equipment. This bridge enabled the weekly Ranger parades to be held in an atmosphere of much greater realism than is usually possible, and added greatly to the attraction of the proceedings. Princess Elizabeth soon gained promotion as "bos'n of the starboard watch", and thoroughly enjoyed all the fun of training both afloat and ashore.

The culmination of her days as a Guide came in March 1945 when it was made known that the Princess had accepted the post of Sea Ranger Commodore of the Girl Guides. This did not mean, however, that she relinquished active association with the movement. Months later, on her first visit alone to Wales, the Princess went to Cardiff to attend and speak at a meeting of the Guides' Council of the Girl Guides' Association for Wales. That night, Princess Elizabeth went up into the hills to the Guides' camp, sat with them round the campfire, and joined in their singsong after supper.

That was one of the last occasions on which the Princess took part in a gathering of Guides as one of them. When she attended the Guides' parade in Hyde Park just after her twentieth birthday, it was more formally, in her capacity as Commodore, and she stood rightly apart from the other girls, taking the two-fingered Guide salute from them as they marched past her. But for a holiday week later in the year, she went again with Ranger friends for training aboard an M.T.B. on the River Dart.

In the Guides, the Princess also met girls from other environments than her own. Though her Kingfisher Patrol companions were mostly daughters of Court officials or of friends of her parents, the crew of the *Duke of York*, as her Sea Rangers ship was later called, made up a cross section of the community, and included a typist, a clerk, a nursemaid, an hotel receptionist, and a groom's daughter.

The Guides' training had fulfilled its purpose. It had definitely added to the equipment, mental, psychological and spiritual, with which the Princess faced the opening of a new life of service, and the Guide law, with its promises to "do her duty to God and the King and to help other people at all times" defines an attitude towards life which she had adopted very much as her own.

Princess Elizabeth rides for the first time with her father at the Trooping the Colour parade in honour of the King's official birthday. With them is the Duke of Gloucester.

CHAPTER EIGHT

"H.R.H. the Colonel"

ON her sixteenth birthday, Princess Elizabeth was appointed by the King to be Colonel of the First, or Grenadier Guards. This was the first fully official appointment under the Crown to be given to the Princess, the other post which she already held, that of President of the Royal College of Music, ranking as a public, but not a Crown, appointment.

To the Princess, this birthday gift was a matter for great rejoicing. It marked a definite stage in her advance towards womanhood and emancipation from the nursery, and she regarded it accordingly with feelings of pride and pleasure, and a determination to do whatever lay within her powers to identify herself with her regiment. To the Grenadiers, also, the King's decision was a matter for rejoicing, for it bound them by yet another tie to the Royal House, and this time to the chief representative of the youngest generation of it, in the person of the heiress-presumptive. At that time, officers and men of the three regular battalions of the regiment, after fighting with the expeditionary force in France as bitterly and hard as ever the regiment had fought in the course of its three hundred years of history, and gaining new glory amid the darkness of Dunkirk, were preparing for a new onslaught against the Germans, with three more war battalions training with them, just ready to go overseas for the start of the long campaign that led them through Africa, Italy, France, Holland and Germany.

With this in their minds, there were not wanting people who, looking at the matter very superficially, thought there was something incongruous in the placing of a young inexperienced girl of sixteen as the titular head of the senior regiment of the world-renowned Brigade of Guards. Such thoughts were strictly confined to people outside the Brigade, who had never taken the trouble to acquaint themselves with its history, for the Princess, though she might be the first woman Colonel of the Grenadiers, was by no means the first Colonel of Royal rank. Nor was the appointment, as some people wrongly supposed, an "honorary" one. True, the Princess could not command the regiment in the field, nor could she reasonably be expected to take an active part in the administrative and training duties of the battalions. But she was, and still is, the actual and active Colonel of the regiment, with clearly defined duties and obligations devolving upon her, duties which, in the six years that have passed since then, she has carried out with careful attention.

To understand this position, it is necessary to know something of the peculiar formation of the command in the five regiments of His Majesty's Footguards, of which the Grenadiers are first, the Coldstream second, the Scots Guards third, the Irish Guards fourth, and the Welsh Guards, created in the 1914–18 war, fifth. In supreme command of the Brigade always is the reigning Sovereign, who is Colonel-in-Chief of each and all the five regiments. Under him are five Colonels chosen from members of the Royal family, and figures of more than ordinary military distinction, each of whom is Colonel of one particular regiment. Thus the Duke of Gloucester is the present Colonel of the Scots Guards, a position held by the King before his accession. But the five Colonels do not usually do full-time duty with their regiments, which alike in the barracks and in the field are commanded by an officer who, while holding the rank of full colonel, and wearing the crown and two stars that are the shoulder insignia of that rank, is known as the "*Lieutenant-Colonel Commanding*". Under him, in each of the five regiments, are officers of the rank of lieutenant-colonel, in command of the various battalions. They are always referred to in the Brigade as "the Commanding Officer", never as "the (Lieutenant-) Colonel".

Like most other of the queer-seeming paradoxes in British military nomenclature, this is the result of no mere whim or chance, but marks the continuance in an unbroken tradition of a practice which started when Charles II formed the Grenadier Guards in 1656. In that year, Charles, still in exile, raised a regiment from the gentlemen who had followed him, and called it the "Royal Regiment of Guards". Thomas, fourth Baron Wentworth, who formed and commanded the regiment, found that he had other duties claiming too much of his time to allow him adequately and fully to carry out his duties at the head of the Guards, so he appointed another officer to carry them out in his stead. This officer holding the place of the Colonel while he was away was properly called the "Lieutenant-Colonel", since he "held the place" of the Colonel: and so he has remained through the long line of Colonels stretching from the loyal Lord Wentworth of three centuries ago to Princess Elizabeth to-day.

The Princess's immediate predecessor as Colonel of the Grenadiers was her own great-great uncle, Queen Victoria's youngest son, Field Marshal the Duke of Connaught, who held the post up to his death at the age of ninety-two in 1942. Before him, the Colonel was another Royal soldier, the Duke of Cambridge, last Royal Commander-in-Chief of the British Army, and before him Albert, the Prince Consort. Princess Elizabeth's appointment as Colonel, therefore, far from being ill-fitting to the fame of the incomparable Grenadiers, was exactly the reverse, illustrating the intimate and long association of the regiment with the person of the Sovereign precisely at a time when the Grenadiers were giving doughty battle in the name of their King to the King's enemies. And the Grenadiers were proud that the King had shown his confidence in them by giving their Colonelcy to his elder daughter as her first post.

As a mark and remembrance of the occasion, the officers of the regiment subscribed for a presentation to their new Royal Colonel, in the form of a diamond brooch, shaped to represent the regimental badge of the Royal Cipher reversed and interlaced.

Colonel John Prescott, "Lieutenant-Colonel Commanding", had handed Princess Elizabeth the brooch before the parade in the quadrangle of Windsor Castle on her birthday, and she scored her first success as a public speaker when she made a short, unexpected, and entirely impromptu speech of thanks—a charming gesture all the more appreciated because of its spontaneity. Since then, the Princess has worn the diamond brooch in the lapel of her coat and the small gilt flaming grenade cap badge of an officer in her hat whenever she has visited her regiment, or taken part in any function connected with the Brigade of Guards.

One small point about that birthday parade, unnoticed by most observers, is worthy of record. For the first time, as they walked round the lines together, Princess Elizabeth

A tribute to the Colonel-in-Chief: a small "daughter of the Regiment" gives the Princess a bouquet on a visit to the 16th/5th Lancers.

went in front of her father—she, and not His Majesty the Colonel-in-Chief, was the inspecting officer.

When the Princess attained her eighteenth birthday, the officers of the Grenadier Guards decided to give her another present that would serve to mark even more closely her position at their head. In olden days, the Colonel always had a Colour of his own, though this practice had been allowed to lapse many years before, and the King's permission was sought, and very readily obtained, to revive the old custom by presenting the Princess with a Colour of her own, to be known as "H.R.H. Princess Elizabeth's Colour", and to be mounted whenever the Royal Colonel was present in person. The King took a close interest in the proposal, personally suggesting an alteration in the design, by placing the Princess's monogram embroidered in each corner of the Colour. By the time April 21 came round again, and the tall Guardsmen, spick and span in the khaki battledress they contrived to imbue with a smartness to be equalled nowhere outside the Brigade, were drawn up for the birthday parade in the Grand Quadrangle at Windsor Castle, the Colour had left the embroiderers' hands, and stood, still furled in its case, in the charge of a young officer.

Colonel Prescott saluted the Princess as she went forward alone between the old and the new King's Guard—both on this momentous regimental occasion drawn from the Grenadiers—to receive her Colour from him. Dressed in a coat of hyacinth blue with a peaked hat in her own "Guards style" the Princess bore herself so well, accepting the

Colour with such grace and dignity, thanking the "Lieutenant-Colonel Commanding" with such a friendly smile, that two groups of officers, one Canadian, the other American, who were watching from inside the quadrangle railings, had difficulty in refraining from cheers. As the Princess walked past the ranks of khaki-clad, steel-helmeted Grenadiers, not a Guardsman moved his eyes: but not a Guardsman missed seeing that in the lapel of her coat she wore the diamond badge of the regiment given her two years beforehand. They notice things like that, in the Guards. This time the King remained on the saluting dais, leaving his daughter to carry out her inspection as Colonel on her own.

The Princess's Colour is a reproduction in miniature of the King's Colour of the First Battalion. It measures nineteen inches by twenty-one, and is of crimson silk, with the Crown embroidered in colours and gold thread. It has a gold fringe and a gold and crimson cord and tassel.

It differs from the King's Colour in two respects. The battle honours of the First Battalion are omitted, owing to the smaller size of the Princess's Colour, and in each corner, by the "desire"—according to the official description of the Colour—"of His Majesty, the Colonel-in-Chief of the Regiment, there appears, in gold thread, H.R.H.'s monogram, surmounted by her coronet"—an interesting example of the detailed attention which the King pays to all such questions of military and heraldic procedure. The coronets follow a design provided by Garter King of Arms from the coronet that appears on the Royal Warrant of the Princess's Arms.

Again, it is to King Charles II that we have to go to trace the history of the Colonel's Colour. That monarch decreed that the King's Colour of the First Battalion should be the Colonel's "proper"—or, in the modern phrase, "own"—Colour. He directed that the Colour should be of white silk, with a cross of crimson silk throughout, differenced with the Imperial Crown in gold. Charles's brother, James II, changed this design soon after his accession, ordering that his own Company's Colour, and the Colonel's Colour, should be of crimson silk instead of white. Nearly two hundred years later, the allocation of this Colour to the Colonel of the Regiment was confirmed by Queen Victoria, and in an issue of regimental orders for March 26, of 1885, it is stated: "The Colonel's Colour will always be taken as the Queen's Colour of the First Battalion."

This Colour, it must be pointed out, is entirely different from the Princess's personal standard which is flown to signify her presence on many formal official occasions

The Royal Colonel-in-Chief arrives for an inspection of the 16th/5th Lancers before the Regiment went overseas.

"H.R.H. The Colonel" inspects the big drum: an incident during a visit to the 2nd Batn. Grenadier Guards.

when her father and mother are not present. Her Colour as Colonel of the Grenadier Guards is also flown to indicate her personal presence, and must not be mounted except when she is on parade. But it is purely a regimental symbol, and is never used on any occasion, military or civil, other than parades or inspections of the Grenadiers.

At Windsor Castle, after the Colour had been presented to the Princess, the King, who never fails to interpret the feeling of a crowd, suggested that it should be carried round for the guests, officers of other regiments, wives, relations and friends of Grenadier officers and men, to see, and Sergeant-Major Douglas proudly carried the new Colour round the quadrangle for everyone to examine, and to admire the intricate needlework and embroidery of the Colour, in which complete accuracy of colour was demanded.

One feature of Princess Elizabeth's tenure of the Colonelcy is unique in all the long history of the regiment. Just before she was first appointed, her own cousin, the Princess Royal's elder son, Viscount Lascelles, then eighteen, had joined her regiment—which was also his father's old one—in the ranks as a Guardsman, as no other past or present member of the Royal family had ever done. It was not until November 1942 that he received his commission after he had served the necessary months as a cadet, so that for six months the Royal Colonel had her Royal first cousin serving in the ranks of her regiment as a private, a strange position brought about by the new democratic rules of entry for officers, and one which Charles II could never even have imagined when he first formed the regiment. As an officer, Lord Lascelles—now the Earl of Harewood—fought with distinction in the Italian campaign until he was captured by the Germans outside Perugia, leading a patrol near Monte Corneo in June 1944.

Not only on formal parades in honour of her own birthday, but on many other occasions of different kinds, grave and gay, and in many other ways, the Princess has identified herself with the regiment. Perhaps her greatest moment came quite early in her career as Colonel, when, a week before her seventeenth birthday, she went off on her own for the very first time, to inspect a battalion of the Grenadiers stationed "somewhere in Southern Command", motoring over to them from Badminton, where she was staying on a short visit to Queen Mary. What made this visit specially exciting for the young Colonel was that the battalion she inspected was a Guards tank battalion, part of that magnificent formation which fought so brilliantly in Holland eighteen months later, the Guards

Armoured Division. Existence of such a Division was still a secret, its symbol of a human eye, flanked in the familiar blue-and-red Brigade colours, which the Princess saw adorning each of the line of tanks, and sewn on the sleeve of each Guardsman's tunic, remaining to the outside world just another of the many mysterious badges and flashes which they saw but did not understand, and the Princess felt a certain justifiable pride in thus being made free of her first war secret. To show her that, even under modern conditions of war, the Grenadiers did not intend to allow such matters as mechanisation and camouflage to interrupt the regimental traditions of drill and soldierly smartness, the tank crews paraded to receive the Royal Colonel with all the precision of line and movement that has gained them the title of the finest foot soldiers in the world. The whole battalion presented arms in the Royal salute with a simultaneous clash of rifles, which the Princess, standing alone on a dais, acknowledged with a slight inclination of her head, and a smile—the form of military "salute" which she worked out for herself, and has since kept for use on all such occasions.

When the Guards had marched past her to the strain of "The British Grenadiers", officers led the Princess over to inspect the tanks.

Never before had the Guards had any direct connection with these queer pieces of self-propelled armoury, but in the short time since the Armoured Division had been organised, the Grenadiers, at any rate, had contrived to put something of the Guards spirit even into their tanks. Dull and ugly their outsides might have to be with camouflage, but inside the tank, as she peered down through the open turret after clambering up onto

In khaki battledress or scarlet tunics the Guards parade with equal smartness: the Princess inspecting her regiment at Caterham depot.

the top of one, the Princess could see every item of equipment polished and shining in true Guards style. And, as she drove to lunch in the officers' mess, the Princess noted, with some inward amusement, that the carefully camouflaged staff car in which she rode had been given a high polish till its dull khaki paintwork shone with almost a Motor Show finish. As soon as the battalion went into action, of course, all that polish would be worse than useless, for it enabled the car to be picked out miles away as it caught the spring sunshine. But until that time came, a polished car certainly looked smarter, so polished it was, and so were many of the other staff cars which bore the "Eye" sign: and they remained polished until the Division moved to its concentration areas before going overseas.

A year later, in March 1944, the Princess saw more of the Guards Armoured Division at the time when preparations for the coming "D-Day" were at their height. It was her first visit to the invading Army of Liberation, and she was thrilled, as no one who saw them could help being thrilled, at the proud bearing and confident spirits of the troops, among whom none were prouder or more confident than the Guards.

This time she showed that she had evidently been thinking about tanks and their peculiar ways in the interval since her last visit, by asking a young officer in command of a Sherman tank the baffling question, "Which part of the track is stationary when a tank is moving forward?"—a question that has been hotly argued in tank "harbours" before and after battle wherever tanks have fought. Princess Elizabeth told the officer she knew from experience that you can put your foot on the bottom of the track, and prove that it stands still while the tank goes forward, but she wanted to know the scientific explanation of the apparent paradox. Unfortunately—or perhaps fortunately for the officer concerned—the Royal party moved on, and the Princess had to follow her father and mother before her curiosity had been satisfied.

On this tour, the Princess saw another aspect of the Guards' way with tanks, watching the squadrons wheel and form into line and change positions with all the accuracy, though little of the grace, of a detachment of the Royal Horse Guards or the Life Guards on their chargers. She herself, with the King and Queen, was several times a passenger in jeeps and half-track scout cars which took them across the tank-ploughed fields to vantage points to watch the training.

Nearer D-Day, Princess Elizabeth inspected two further battalions of the Grenadiers, bidding them God speed in the great ordeal she knew was just before them: though even the Princess did not know when the invasion was to be launched.

Later on, when some of the Guards had come marching home again, with another series of victories to be inscribed on the regimental colours, the Princess said good-bye to the first of the Grenadier war battalions to be disbanded, the Fifth Battalion, which had fought in the African campaign, and in Italy from Anzio—where the Commanding Officer was killed—onwards. The farewell parade at Wellington Barracks was arranged some time in advance for a particular date in May; and no more appropriate date could have been chosen, for, as it happened, it was on May 7, the eve of VE-Day, that the Princess drove through the thronging crowds round the Palace gates to the barracks. Her farewell to the Fifth Battalion was therefore her last public appearance before the end of the war in Europe, and when, addressing the parade after a march past, she said, "It is fitting before you disperse you should be able to see victory assured . . ." she paused,

*The Royal Colonel inspects her regiment.
The Argyll and Sutherland Highlanders
on parade at the ancient Scottish capital
of Stirling.*

looked up, and smiled at the understatement, knowing that at the Palace her father was still awaiting word from Downing Street to proclaim victory that night or the next.

Since then, the Princess has visited the Grenadiers at training at the Caterham depot where so many good Guardsmen have been made: at Windsor: and at Hawick. She has made all the regiment's interests her own, the welfare of widows of Grenadiers, the Old Comrades' Association, and so on. No call on her time is too much if it is a question of the regiment, and the Lieutenant-Colonel Commanding is a frequently received visitor in her apartments at the Palace or at Windsor Castle. She likes to be kept informed of all that is going on, of awards and decorations won by Grenadiers, and of other regimental matters. When, for instance, she heard that the Ladies' Committee, which looked after the welfare of wives and widows of Grenadiers during the war, was to be disbanded, she insisted on travelling specially to London from Sandringham to attend the final meeting at Wellington Barracks, and to make a presentation herself on behalf of the regiment to the secretary of the committee.

The same night, the Princess went to a private dinner at Claridge's, given in her honour, at which she met some of the senior officers of the other regiments of the Brigade of Guards.

A few days before the great Victory Parade of June 8, 1946, the Princess attended a special parade of the Grenadiers, a parade of the wartime soldiers who had helped to win new renown for the regiment, now lined up with other, older Guardsmen, on the Regimental Remembrance Day, to attend service at Wellington Barracks as members of the Grenadier Guards Comrades' Association, to be inspected by the Princess, to march to the Guards Division Memorial on Horse Guards Parade where their President, Lieut.-General Sir Bertram Sergison-Brooke, laid a wreath, and finally, to march past the Palace, where "H.R.H. the Colonel" stood to take the salute. This meant the giving up of yet another of her few free Sundays: but she made no demur. Her Regiment's claim was paramount. This has become a regular annual event in the Princess's diary: and there is none which she fulfils with greater readiness.

Another notable day in Grenadier history was June 12, 1947, when, at the Trooping the Colour Parade on the King's official birthday, the Princess, as Colonel of the regiment, rode for the first time at her father's side with her brother Colonels. Two other British regiments now count Princess Elizabeth among their officers. On her twenty-first birthday the King appointed her Colonel-in-Chief of the 16th/5th Lancers and the Argyll and Sutherland Highlanders. She is also Colonel-in-Chief of the Railways and Harbours Brigade South African Army, the Royal Durban Light Infantry, and the 48th Highlanders of Canada and the Régiment de la Chaudière.

In days to come her Army interests will widen further. But to her, no other regiment will ever compare with the Grenadiers, the First Regiment of Footguards, and her own first regiment.

CHAPTER NINE

Finances and Household

PRINCESS ELIZABETH, who now, as Heiress Presumptive with a consort and an independent household of her own, commands a yearly income of forty thousand pounds, learned the value of money as a small girl by having no more than a shilling a week pocket money, out of which she was expected to save regularly.

Those early lessons in sound finance, taught her by the Queen, bore good fruit, for, when the young Princess, making one of her very first visits to a public institution, went to the headquarters of the Post Office Savings Bank in Blythe Road Kensington, in 1939, she was delighted to be shown the index card of her own personal account, recording a credit of some thirty pounds. Her accounts to-day are much more complex, but she has imposed an over-all rule, ever since the beginning of her married life, against extravagance and in favour of thrift and well-balanced accounts.

Forty thousand pounds a year sounds, and indeed is, an immense sum even for the heiress to the throne. But closer scrutiny of the Princess's income and finances quickly puts the matter in a very different light. From her yearly allowance, the Princess must make provision in every way for the proper upkeep of the dignity of her position. From it she must pay the salaries of all the members of her official household. She must pay the wages of all the servants at her official and private residences. She must pay fares on trains, ships and aeroplanes whenever and wherever she travels, with the exceptions of passages in His Majesty's ships and aircraft, when, as the daughter of their legal owner, she is naturally entitled to travel free. She must set aside a very large sum each year for the many charitable contributions she is called upon to make. She must set aside another sum for entertainment, for the reception of distinguished Empire and foreign visitors, for official parties of various kinds. She must pay for the upkeep of motor cars and the chauffeurs and staff to run them. She must pay for the upkeep and furnishing of Clarence House, her official residence, as well as for her private home, at Windlesham Moor, Sunningdale. She must, even in these days of coupons, spend a large amount yearly on dress, for as ambassadress-at-large for Britain, she must always appear perfectly turned-out. No figures, even of the most general kind, can be given for the various items, large and small, which go to make up the Princess's yearly budget, but some idea of the total involved in all this official expenditure may be gained from the fact that the Princess Elizabeth's and the Duke of Edinburgh's Annuities Act of 1948, under which she draws her income from the Consolidated Fund, provides that all but four thousand of the forty thousand pounds shall be tax free. This means that the Select Committee of the House, which sat for a long time investigating the whole position before making its recommendations to the Commons, was satisfied that thirty-six thousand pounds a year would be absorbed in official expenditure of one sort or another, and thus was not liable for taxation. On the remaining four thousand pounds, the

Mr. John Colville:
Private Secretary.

Lady Margaret Egerton:
Lady-in-Waiting.

Princess pays income and surtax in accordance with the same provisions as govern the incomes of any of her father's subjects.

Even so, many people may opine that thirty-six thousand pounds is a vast sum to spend under the headings enumerated above. Princess Elizabeth herself probably agrees with them. But to maintain a Royal establishment with fitting dignity, things must be done in royal, if not in extravagant, style. When the Princess travels by train, for example, she cannot merely take a reserved first-class seat in an ordinary carriage, even if she

Lady Margaret Hay:
Lady-in-Waiting.

wished to do so. Instead, she must travel in a special coach, and with her must travel a certain retinue, consisting usually of her secretary or equerry, her lady-in-waiting, her detective, and her maid, for all of whom, including herself, the Princess has to pay full first-class fare, with the added cost of the special coach, all of which adds up to a heavy bill for any single journey—and the Princess normally travels many thousands of miles in the course of a year to fulfil her engagements in various parts of the country. Besides this, there is often the added cost of sending her car in advance by rail, with a chauffeur as well, an item which may seem unnecessary until it is remembered that the Royal cars are specially designed among other things to give people a good view of their occupants. There would quickly be an outcry if the

140

The Hon. Mrs. Andrew Elphinstone:
Extra Lady-in-Waiting.

Lieut.-General Sir Frederick (Boy)
Browning: Comptroller and Treasurer
of the Household.

Princess appeared in the crowd-lined streets of some provincial town, driving in a small local saloon car with little windows.

Most people know nowadays that the King and the other members of the Royal family derive their incomes from a grant out of the national funds. The income of Princess Elizabeth and that of her husband, who receives ten thousand a year to provide independently for his own staff, travelling expenses, and so on, fall within this category. But that is not all the story.

The Civil List annuities are paid to the Crown in return for the placing by each successive Sovereign "unreservedly at the disposal of the House of Commons those hereditary revenues which were so placed by his predecessor", or in other words, for the handing over to the nation of what are known as the Crown Lands, which consist of immensely valuable properties in London and elsewhere. These properties legally descend to the Sovereign's heir: but from the days of George III they have been surrendered in return for an annual payment determined by Parliament. Since the value of the ground rents and other sources of income have increased manyfold in the past two hundred years, the arrangement yields a very large profit to the nation, a profit increased in no small measure during the present reign by the King's magnanimous and spontaneous act in handing to the Exchequer the income of the Duchy of Cornwall, which revert to him while the Dukedom is in abeyance, in the absence of a son of the reigning sovereign. Out of this revenue which amounted to £117,604 in 1936, the annuities of Princess Elizabeth were, by the King's command, paid until her marriage. She received six thousand pounds a year during her minority, out of which all her personal expenses, her clothes, education, and staff were paid. At twenty-one, her income was automatically increased to fifteen thousand pounds to enable her to set up an establishment of her own. But she had enjoyed this grant for only six months when her

A gift from the R.A.F.: the Princess's official motor car, which was bought with money subscribed by the R.A.F. and the W.A.A.F. It is a 27-h.p. limousine.

marriage brought up the whole question for review. To the "faithful Commons", the King sent a message on the eve of his daughter's wedding, "relying on the liberality and affection" of the House, and the "cordial interest" they had manifested in the approaching marriage, and asking that they should give consideration to making provision for "Princess Elizabeth and Lieutenant Mountbatten". The King added an important rider to his request. His Majesty, "Being anxious that this provision should be made in such a way as not to impose a burden on his people at the present time when they are faced with grave economic difficulties, is willing to place at the disposal of the faithful Commons a sum derived from savings on the Civil List during the war years with the intent that the provision made by them should for a period impose no additional charge on the public funds".

The sum handed over by the King was no less than one hundred thousand pounds, a "wedding present" to the nation which provides Princess Elizabeth's additional income for four years, so that it will not be until 1951–2 that the extra twenty-five thousand pounds allocated to the Princess will come to be set off against the profits of the Crown Lands.

When the Select Committee appointed by the House to examine the King's suggestion made their report, Sir Stafford Cripps, as Chancellor of the Exchequer, was able to tell the House that the Committee had shown themselves anxious to reach a unanimous decision, if possible, adding that the differences of opinion which emerged marked the anxiety of all present to reach a compromise arrangement. Differing only on the amount and not the principle involved, five members merely recommended a total five thousand pounds less than the figure agreed by the thirteen who formed the majority. When the report was put to the House, some further divergence of opinion showed itself. One member thought the Royal couple should be asked to put in a fairly detailed account of how they had spent that part of their annuities devoted to official entertaining and other expenses, which another member at once suggested would be placing the Princess and her husband in the position of a reporter putting in a weekly expenses sheet, while a second strange ground for opposing the grant was that it would bring the Royal family into disrepute. Even the member who moved that there should be no increase at all in the allowance paid to the Princess was at pains to point out that he had the best interests of the monarchy at heart, and he and his friends merely wished to "take them out of the gilded cage". His amendment was defeated by the overwhelming majority of 345 votes to 33. Then a second amendment was put, to reduce the amount by five thousand pounds a year, in accordance with the views of the minority of the Committee. This, too, its mover was careful to point out, was an effort in favour of, and not against, the monarchy, to which, he thought, the people of the country would like to attach the adjectives: simple, austere and democratic. But the Commons did not take kindly to the thought of dimming the bright shield of Britain's monarchy with the dull greyness of austerity, however well-intentioned was the motive behind the suggestion, and that amendment was soundly and roundly defeated by 291 votes to 165, the Government permitting a free vote of the House, so that members could vote according to their conscience and not at the dictates of the Party Whips.

To foreigners and those unused to the intricacies of the British system of constitutional monarchy, all this public debate over the amount the nation was to grant its future Queen, not for her own personal pleasure, but for the purpose of maintaining and representing the dignity of the nation and empire, seemed both unnecessary and in poor, if not bad, taste. But open and free discussion of such matters is one of the keystones of democracy, a thing not to be tolerated in totalitarian states, and the courteous references to the Royal couple even by those who supported the amendments can easily stand comparison with the sharper sentences used by members of the House who debated the question of allowances for Queen Victoria's Prince Consort a century before. The importance of the matter is that it shows both the integration of the monarchy with the freely elected Parliament of the land, and the high esteem and respect in which the monarchy to-day is held by members of all parties.

The Act was given the Royal Assent on February 11, 1948.

Until Princess Elizabeth came of age, her finances were administered for her, under the supervision of the Keeper of the King's Privy Purse. Few people outside the Court circle—and not everyone within it—have any idea of how carefully all the Royal funds, including the incomes of minors, are administered, or with what exactitude accounts are checked and balanced. No longer, in these days, can even Royal Palaces be run with that happy disregard for sound finance that was a characteristic of some of our bygone Kings, whose lives of opulent splendour often caused them to resort to rather dubious methods of money-raising. For many years at Buckingham Palace there has been in operation a system of costing which enables the King to know, to a fraction of a penny, just how his moneys are being spent, and in what proportions. Similar business-like methods, replacing the haphazard lack of system of the old days, have been adopted by Princess Elizabeth for the administration of her own household and finances.

It was not until the Princess was eighteen that the first appointment to her official Household was made. Up to that date, her "household" consisted of her governess, Miss Marion Crawford (who married Mr. George Buthlay, a banker, shortly before the Princess married), her chief nurse, Mrs. "Alla" Knight (who died, deeply mourned by the Queen and both Princesses, in 1947), and her personal maid, Miss Margaret Mac-Donald, a quiet-spoken, unobtrusive Scotswoman, who to-day is still with the Princess, to whom she is utterly devoted. The increasing calls on the Princess for official appearances made it necessary for a Lady-in-Waiting to be appointed to her, and not long after her eighteenth birthday, it was announced, on July 10, 1944, that Lady Mary Palmer, the twenty-three-year-old daughter of Lord Selborne, had been appointed by the King as the first member of his daughter's official household. She had been only a few months in the Royal Household when she married Major Anthony Strachey. Next appointment was of another Lady-in-Waiting, this time a young war widow, the Hon. Mrs. Vicary Gibbs, daughter of Captain A. V. Hambro, a member of the well-known banking family. Between her and the Princess, who calls her by her Christian name, Jean, a close friendship grew up. When she married the Princess's cousin, Captain the Hon. Andrew Elphinstone, second son of the Queen's sister, Lady Elphinstone, the Princess attended their wedding with the Queen, and she is godmother to their small daughter.

Third to be appointed to the Princess's Household was Lady Margaret Egerton, sister of the Earl of Ellesmere, slim, attractive, and possessed of a charming smile and an alert sense of humour. Lady Margaret, who is known to all in the Royal circle as "Meg", accompanied the Royal party to South Africa in attendance on the Princesses, and was one of the most popular members of the Royal entourage wherever they went. Among other bonds which link her with her Royal mistress is an interest in the A.T.S., for, like the Princess, Lady Margaret served as an A.T.S. officer during the war. Lady Margaret Seymour, sister of the Marquess of Hertford, was appointed as another Lady-in-Waiting to the Princess in 1947. She married Mr. Philip Hay, son of the late Alan Hay and Mrs. Hay, of Mere, Wiltshire, a year after joining the Household.

The two Lady Margarets were among the hardest worked people at Buckingham Palace in the weeks preceding Princess Elizabeth's wedding, in recognition of which the Princess had them both in attendance on her at the Abbey, where they walked in the bride's procession, immediately behind her eight bridesmaids.

In June, 1947, with the prospect of an early announcement of her engagement to add to the growing volume of her daily business, the Princess decided the time had arrived for her to have a private secretary. Mr. John Rupert Colville, son of the Hon. George Colville, and Lady Cynthia Colville, a lifelong friend of Queen Mary, was chosen for this important and responsible post. Educated at Harrow and Trinity College, Cambridge, Mr. Colville who was born in 1914, joined the Foreign Service, was one of the private secretaries of the late Mr. Neville Chamberlain when he was Prime Minister, and continued in that capacity under Mr. Churchill, serving in the R.A.F. during the war. Dark, of medium stature, with perfect manners and an extremely alert brain, "Jock", as he is known to a very wide circle of friends, is responsible for organising all the details of the Princess's official engagements, and for many other important matters. He sees the Princess at least once every day. In July 1948 he and Lady Margaret Egerton announced their engagement.

As the Comptroller, or head, of her Household, the Princess chose Lieutenant-General Sir Frederick (Boy) Browning, leading spirit in the formation of Britain's airborne troops, and afterwards Commander of the Airborne Invasion troops.

General Browning, who continues in civil life the reputation he gained as the most smartly turned-out officer in the Brigade of Guards—he is a Grenadier—as well as one of the most capable organisers in the Army, is a man of great personal charm. He is general charge of the Household of the Princess and her husband, looking after finances, signing cheques, choosing staff, and supervising all the details of the Royal home. Under his direction, the Princess's household is run with clockwork smoothness and military precision.

Next appointment came after the Princess's marriage, when Lieutenant Michael Parker, a twenty-seven-year-old officer of the Royal Navy, born in Australia of British parents, was chosen as Equerry to both the Princess and the Duke. First man of Australian birth to be appointed to the Royal Household, "Mike" Parker was a wartime friend

Clarence House, St. James's Palace, the official residence of Princess Elizabeth and her husband.

of the Duke of Edinburgh, with whom he served in destroyers on the East Coast Patrol. Some months later, a second Equerry, Squadron-Leader Philip Arnott, a wartime fighter pilot with a double D.F.C., was appointed to the Princess and the Duke, thus completing the representation of the three Services in their Household.

One other important person attached to the Princess's Household is Inspector Alec Usher, of "A" Division, Metropolitan Police. Chosen as police guard for the Princess when she first began to undertake engagements outside London, Inspector Usher was appointed as permanent officer attached to her in June, 1947. Like everyone else directly or indirectly in her service, Usher, who goes everywhere with the Princess, has a tremendous regard and esteem for her.

Though the Princess had a Household when she married, she had to start her married life without a home of her own. The King gave her Sunninghill Park, a big twenty-five-roomed house near Windsor, soon after her engagement. But a disastrous fire, which broke out only a fortnight later, almost completely destroyed the big house, and post-war conditions made restoration out of the question, at any rate for some years. Clarence House, in St. James's Palace, was bestowed by the King on his daughter as her town house, but here, too, labour and material shortages prevented the old-fashioned house, which had last been inhabited by the veteran Duke of Connaught who died in 1942, from being altered and re-decorated in time for the Princess and her husband to take up residence after their honeymoon. Like Sunninghill Park, Clarence House was given to the Princess as a "grace and favour" residence. So extensive were the necessary alterations and decorations at Clarence House that the Office of Works architects had to plan for a full year's work before it could be ready. The history of Clarence House, built originally for the Princess's great-great-great-granduncle, the Duke of Clarence, afterwards William IV, makes it a particularly fitting dwelling for the Heiress Presumptive and her consort. In an old Warrant Book in the Lord Chamberlain's Office, it is described as "The Queen's House", though there is no existing record of any Queen having lived there.

As a substitute for Sunninghill Park, the Princess and the Duke took over on lease an attractive, very comfortable modern house, Windlesham Moor, at Sunningdale, whose owner, by coincidence, is Mrs. Warwick Bryant, widow of the former owner of Sunninghill Park. In London, they made their headquarters at Buckingham Palace, occupying the suite of rooms that had been the Princess's before marriage, until Clarence House could be made ready for them.

One other house remains the Princess's property, though she can never enter it again herself. It is "Y Bwthyn Bach", "The Little House", given her by the people of Wales when she was six years old. It still stands, unoccupied, in the grounds of The Royal Lodge, the King's home in Windsor Great Park. Perhaps the Princess's children one day will fill its small rooms with laughter again.

In this crinoline-skirted evening robe of richly-embroidered silk, with off-the-shoulder top, the Princess won Parisian hearts by her charm. She is wearing the red ribbon of the Grand Cross of the Legion of Honour, which had just been bestowed on her by the French President. The Duke wears the Order of the Garter, of which he is the youngest Knight.

CHAPTER TEN

The Princess and Her Clothes

DRESS, important to all women, is all the more important to Princesses, so much of whose lives must perforce be spent in public, where their appearance, their manner, and above all, their dress, form the target for a thousand curious eyes. They, more than other women of high degree or low, must take care to dress in good taste, neither to appear so often in different clothes of ultra-fashionable cut as to risk the accusation of ostentation, nor to be so indifferent to appearance as to cause criticism on the opposite score. Those considerations have applied to Princesses in all ages. In our present age of shortages and coupons, the course between the two extremes is even more difficult to follow, for some envious folk are not wanting who will assess every new dress that Royalty may wear in terms of coupon value.

Princess Elizabeth, with her innate good sense, has found no difficulty in avoiding both these two pitfalls.

As a young girl, and in the days when she first began to go about in public, she manifested no great interest in clothes, though there were not wanting signs, even in those early days, of the good taste and impeccable dress sense she so abundantly shows to-day. It was a hat, a very simple hat, that first told the outside world that the Princess certainly possessed the first essential of good taste in dress, a knowledge of what is fitting for the occasion: and it was this same hat that first gave evidence of the tremendous impact of the Princess's choice on the fashions of the day. The hat in question was of green felt, brimless, shaped like a beret, with the top jutting a little forward over a small peak to give the effect of a military cap. That was precisely the effect required, for the occasion in question was the Princess's first appearance on parade as Colonel of the Grenadier Guards, on her sixteenth birthday, at Windsor Castle. The Princess wore it with a double-breasted coat, cut on semi-military lines, and everyone who saw her on parade remarked on the appropriateness of her costume, particularly as she wore the flaming grenade cap badge of an officer of the Grenadiers in her hat. Signs of the Princess's influence on the world of fashion came next day when photographs of her appeared in the newspapers. A demand for "Princess hats" sprang up immediately, and copies of her model became best-sellers almost overnight.

It was another Guards occasion, five years later, that gave the Princess an unusual opportunity for showing once again her instinctive ability to choose the right clothes to wear. This time, the problem was not as simple as before, for it was an occasion of full state, the Trooping the Colour parade in honour of the King's official birthday. For the first time, the Princess was to ride in procession with her father and other high-ranking officers of the Brigade from Buckingham Palace to Horse Guards Parade, and to take part with the King and the Duke of Gloucester (Colonel of the Scots Guards) in the trooping ceremony. There were no precedents to guide her since the days of Queen

In Paris: the Princess and the Duke leaving the British Embassy to attend Sunday morning service.

Victoria, who, it is recorded, wore semi-military uniform with a buttoned tunic and a pill-box hat when she reviewed her Volunteers in Hyde Park, and "the uniform of a Field Marshal"—unfortunately, no details are on record—when she reviewed her soldiers after the Crimean War. But it was as an officer of the Guards that the Princess was parading, so she set herself to evolve, with the aid of experts, a costume that would at the same time fit the setting yet not look like a stagey imitation of Guards uniform. There was a good deal of public speculation about what she would wear, for no inkling of her intentions had been allowed to leak out in advance. When she rode out of the gates of the Palace, behind her father, who wore the uniform of Colonel-in-Chief of the Coldstream Guards, it was a delight to see how charmingly she had solved the problem. She wore a military style belted tunic with brass buttons, and the insignia of her rank as a full Colonel on the shoulder straps; a peaked Guards cap, with the Grenadiers badge; and a habit-skirt, all made from the regulation dark blue undress uniform cloth of the Guards Brigade. No one, not even the crustiest of veteran officers of the Brigade, could but acknowledge the rightness of the Princess's choice. The watching crowds, with less concern for the minutiae of military correctness, were delighted, too, for it was the general opinion of soldiers and civilians alike that the Princess had never worn anything more becoming.

The same unerring sense of what is appropriate guides the Princess in her choice of more ordinary, everyday wear. In this, her greatest opportunity—and her greatest test—came on her visit to Paris at Whitsun, 1948. She went from England to the City of Fashion with a wardrobe limited in extent, but chosen with such taste and skill that Parisians everywhere acclaimed the "chic" of the English Princess. They, and a good many people at home, were surprised at the brilliance, for such a strong word is justified here, of the Princess's success. As a fundamental guide for her Paris wardrobe, Princess Elizabeth remained true to her own long-observed rule of avoiding extremes. She eschewed both the exaggerations of the full "New Look" and the demoded short skirts and severity of the old. The resultant compromise was a happy combination of the soft femininity and elegance of the new style with the more practical suitability of the old. Paris, where the New Look itself originated, lost no time in christening the Princess's style as the "Elizabeth Look". Leading fashion houses sent their most expert observers to watch the Princess, to note details of her dresses, her hats, her handbags, her shoes.

Elegance is the keynote of this Royal picture from Paris. Princess Elizabeth walks gracefully down the steps of the Elysée Palace, residence of the French Presidents, after attending a reception given in honour of her and her husband by President Auriol. Her long-skirted evening gown is of heavy silk, she wears long white kid gloves, a tiara of diamonds, and a cape of white fur. Her toeless shoes are of silver, and she carries a white embroidered bag. The Duke of Edinburgh remains a little in the rear as they make their official departure.

The experts' reports were so enthusiastic that models based on the Princess's modes were put in hand at once. The hemline of her afternoon frocks, several inches from the floor, set a new fashion for slightly shorter skirts than the famous couturiers were making. Like all the Princess's ideas, this one had its practical side in checking the tendency to skirts so long that they sweep the floor.

One of the dresses which Paris acclaimed most was a lovely coat-frock in Ottoman silk of a most unusual shade of slate blue, which delighted Londoners, in turn, when she made her first State drive through the City since her marriage, accompanying the Duke of Edinburgh to Guildhall when he was made a Freeman. It has a wide, swirling skirt, a tightened waistline, and large draped pockets. With it, the Princess wore a wide-brimmed bonnet-hat of exactly matching straw, trimmed with tulle, and ankle-strapped platform shoes. The whole effect was delightful in its delicacy and charm.

Another of her gowns which drew gasps of admiration from the watching Parisians was the evening dress she wore to attend a dinner given in her honour by M. Auriol, the President of the Republic, at the Elysée Palace. It was of white satin, decolleté, and off-the-shoulders, trimmed in glittering paillettes and beads of turquoise blue, with the long skirt split in the front to reveal an under-petticoat of the same exquisite shade of blue.

For her Paris visit, the Princess had a special allowance of clothing coupons from the Board of Trade, as was only proper, since she went not as an ordinary holiday visitor but as an Ambassadress from Britain, representing in the eyes of the French the people of their old friend, neighbour and ally. What clothes she wore, with the focus of all French eyes upon her, were a proclamation of British fashion, and the export drive would scarcely have been likely to benefit had the Heiress Presumptive visited Paris wearing dresses of yesterday's styles. Similarly, she received extra coupons for her visit to South Africa with the King and Queen, and for her marriage, too, an extra one hundred coupons were given her. But apart from these occasions, the Princess has confined herself strictly to the normal issue of coupons, utilising them with great ingenuity to make a small wardrobe appear extensive. A gesture that touched her warm heart was at the time of her approaching wedding, when from women all over the country, poor women and rich, came offerings of precious clothing coupons. Many well-meaning folk sent coupons to her at the Palace, others offered their whole books. Princess Elizabeth declined the gifts

*The coronet she wore only once. The
Princess in coronation attire.*

In the dress that charmed Paris. Princess Elizabeth opening the Exhibition of British Life. Seven microphones pick up her words.

with real gratitude, knowing well at what great personal sacrifice they had been offered.

Her wardrobe to-day contains several beautiful garments which have come to her coupon-free, the fur coats from Canada, Newfoundland, and the Hudson Bay Company among them. Dress lengths in rich silks from the East were among her wedding gifts, so, too, were thirty pairs of gloves from the Glovers Company of London: half the number, by order of the Board of Trade, of the Company's traditional present of sixty pairs to Royalty on marriage. Twenty dresses, too, were sent to the Princess from New York, as a wedding gift: but these she gave away, choosing, as their recipients, girls of her own age who were married on her wedding day or near it.

Of all the dresses a woman may wear in her life, it is her wedding dress that commands her greatest interest. In Princess Elizabeth's case, it was of interest not only to the bride herself, but the whole, or nearly the whole, of the outside world. Because she wanted the simple pleasure of keeping her wedding dress a secret until her wedding morning, she gave orders that no details were to be released, no sketches or photographs published, until that happy day. American dress houses, scenting a Royal mystery where none

The Princesses go dancing. Princess Elizabeth's gown of brocaded silk is cut with a long skirt and an off-the-shoulder bodice.

existed, sent fashion spies over, prepared to go to almost any lengths to secure information about the dress. Their object, it was said, was to flood the market with copies of the Royal wedding dress before the Royal wedding. Those in the know, including the scores of girls who worked long hours stitching on the thousands and thousands of pearls and beads which formed part of the embroidery, smiled at the suggestion. The Princess's gown was one of such intricate design, calling for such an immense amount of handwork, that to reproduce it in multiple copies was a sheer impossibility, as the sleuths from over the Atlantic found as soon as they saw the dress or read descriptions of it. Interest in the dress remained, even increased, after the wedding. When it was exhibited at St. James's Palace afterwards, a total of 261,832 people paid to see it, the receipts going to charities named by the Princess. Edinburgh, Cardiff, and Belfast asked for it to be sent for exhibition, and in Edinburgh alone a total of five thousand pounds was collected for the Lifeboat Fund as a result. With the blessing of the Board of Trade, copies were made to send on tour in the Dominions and the United States. Indeed, it is doubtful whether any other wedding dress in history has evoked quite so much or so continued interest.

Princess Elizabeth chose her bridal gown from a score of designs sent to her at Buckingham Palace. Basically, the design of her dress was simple. It was of ivory duchess satin, with a tight fitting bodice, long tight sleeves, a heart-shaped neckline, and a full falling skirt. What gave it that ethereal quality which made the Princess look so much as though she had stepped straight from the pages of a fairy story was the embroidery of pearl and crystal patterned in exquisite magnificence over the skirt and the long fifteen-foot Court train of transparent ivory silk tulle. Mr. Norman Hartnell, who created the dress, found his inspiration for the design in the paintings of Botticelli. The pointed waistline was formed by a girdle of pearl-embroidered star flowers; seed pearls and crystals were hand-stitched, too, in a delicate pattern about the neckline. Garlands of white York roses, emblem of the bride's original rank as Princess of York, carried out in raised pearls, were entwined with ears of corn minutely embroidered in crystals and oat-shaped pearls, patterning the skirt with gleaming beauty. Orange blossom, the traditional flower of a happy bride, found its place in a deep border round the entire hem of the skirt, mingled with star flowers appliqué with transparent tulle bordered with seed pearls and crystals. The long train, too, was exquisite with embroidery in similar design. Of transparent ivory silk tulle, it flowed from the shoulders in a sweeping fan. Satin star flowers, roses and ears of corn were repeated in reverse, the centres of the flowers filled with the silk of the dress. Each of the scores of thousands of pearls and beads was threaded by hand, a work of skill and craftsmanship that, for comparison, sends us back to the spacious elegance of the days of Botticelli and the Renaissance. Seven whole weeks were spent in the making of the dress, with a team of three hundred and fifty girls proud to work long hours every day to have the Princess's gown ready in time. For her veil, the Princess departed from the traditional lace of Royal brides, and chose one of white tulle, held in place by a tiara of diamonds and pearls, which blended beautifully with the pearl-encrusted loveliness of the gown.

The Princess's dislike of the sensational or extravagant in matters of dress was shown in her choice for her going-away dress, for which she selected that pleasant shade of blue known as "love-in-the-mist" which is the choice of so many brides. Her dress of

crêpe in this becoming colour—which has always been one of her favourite shades—was simply cut with a cross-over bodice draped to the left hip, and a straight skirt with twin panels let in on one side, and a hemline fourteen inches from the ground. With this, she wore a coat of exactly the same shade, in velure cloth with soft revers and rounded shoulders to give the new fashion line. Inset bands across the coat front were held with three buttons to the waist, where the skirt flared gently out to fullness.

On her wedding day, the Princess wore, for the first time in her life, really high-heeled shoes. They had the modern platform soles with heels two and three-eighths inches high. Hitherto, Princess Elizabeth had avoided high heels, both because of the greater comfort on the many occasions when her official duties involve, as they so often do, a great deal of walking and standing, and because, again, of her dislike of extreme fashions. For her wedding attire, those advising her unanimously declared high heels were really necessary; and the Princess, who is always ready to sink her own desires when she has been once convinced to the contrary, agreed. The shoes were open-toe sandals in ivory duchess satin, the same material as the wedding dress, finished with silver buckles studded with pearls.

Her going-away hat was a high bonnet on her favourite beret lines,

The Princess in one of the simply-cut, elegant evening gowns that she wears with such grace.

made in mist-blue felt and trimmed with a large pom-pom of ostrich feathers and curved quills in two tones of blue.

Those are details of two of the Princess's most important choices of dress. They give some indication of her general taste in this matter. Her three golden rules for dressing are that her clothes must be becoming, comfortable, and not startling.

Some of the absurd "creations" to be seen in the Royal Enclosure at Ascot, for example, fill the Princess with nothing but disdain. Fully conscious of the importance of her role as fashion ambassadress of Britain, she continues to dress not to please the fashion designers but to please herself, and, because she has such good taste, her choice finds general acceptance. The dress she chose for another occasion of more than ordinary importance, the Silver Wedding of her parents, shows her preference for plain colours in soft shades. This dress was in a delicate shade of china blue, in thick-ribbed silk, with a high-necked bodice embroidered with a panel of white china beads from throat to waistline. Contrasting with the fitted bodice was a flowing, full skirt. Choice of accessories, furs, gloves, handbag, shoes, is as important a factor in good dress as the choice of the dress itself. In this, too, Princess Elizabeth's taste is impeccable. Her hats are chosen with immense care to go with her clothes, while she always remembers the necessity, if they are to be worn on public occasions, of avoiding shapes which will hide her face.

Were coupons to be abolished, and free choice of materials be restored, Princess Elizabeth would not greatly increase her wardrobe. She is no believer in dress for the sake of dressing. From her very early days, when she was brought up to the tidy habit of brushing her own clothes and putting them away herself, she has taken great care of her clothes. To-day, when this responsibility falls on "Bo-Bo", as the Princess affectionately calls her maid, Margaret MacDonald, she still takes a very close interest in the state of her wardrobe, and sees that her clothes are regularly pressed and cleaned. In South Africa, the continual freshness of the Princess's appearance, whether she was wearing formal evening attire for a State function, a silk day frock for a garden party, or jodhpurs and a silk shirt for an early morning ride, was a source of wonder throughout the months-long journey across the Union. For that, most of the credit goes, naturally, to Miss MacDonald, who worked long hours in the confined space of the Royal pressing-cabins aboard the White Train, to ensure that her Royal mistress should always be immaculately turned-out. But part of the credit, too, is due to Princess Elizabeth herself, for the unremitting care she took with her appearance, day after day, in the heat of the South African sunshine.

Four fur coats, which form the most valuable items in the Princess's wardrobe to-day, are all wedding gifts. One, a full-length grey-brown beaver, made in the lightest skins obtainable, was a gift from the "Governor and Adventurers" of the Hudson Bay Company; a second, of most beautiful mink, also full length, was Canada's gift; a third, an evening wrap, also in lovely mink, was given by New Zealand; and a fourth, a cape of grey chinchilla rabbit, made to hip length, came from the British Rabbit-skin Industry, and is formed from thirty matched skins offered by small "backyard" breeders all over the country. Another lovely garment that was a wedding gift is an evening cape in ostrich feathers sent her by the South African Ostrich Farmers Association. It is dyed in the Princess's favourite shade of lime green.

A picture that shows the loveliness of the Princess's wedding dress and richly embroidered train, as she stands in the Throne Room of the Palace with her husband immediately after their return from the Abbey.

CHAPTER ELEVEN

Romance and Marriage—The Royal Wedding in which the whole world joined

THURSDAY, November 20, 1947, was a day which will long be remembered by millions who, through the magic of radio, joined in the marriage service of Princess Elizabeth, Heiress Presumptive to the British Throne, when she married the man of her heart's choice, His Royal Highness Prince Philip, Duke of Edinburgh, Earl of Merioneth, and Baron Greenwich. By the wise and kindly decision of the King, the whole of the wedding service of Westminster Abbey, including the taking of the marriage vows by the Royal couple, was broadcast, an innovation in Royal wedding arrangements which was most happily in keeping with the spirit of the times, and one which enabled men and women of all degrees in nearly every part of the world to share directly for the first time in a Royal marriage service. Nothing that had happened for a score of years, not even the Coronation ceremony itself, perhaps, had given such a sense of personal contact between people and Throne. Nor has any other marriage, of Royalty or commoner, so captured the imagination of the world. The clear contralto voice of Princess Elizabeth uttering the simple, binding words of avowal, "I will", the deeper tones of the Duke's voice—which few listeners had heard before—taking the same loving oath with moving sincerity, touched hearts all over the world, in the distant lands of the Empire, in the United States of America, where hundreds of thousands rose at five-thirty in the morning to hear the service, and in many other lands far and near. In the East End of London, women workers at a factory threatened to quit their machines if the broadcast were not relayed to them. At sea, passengers on the great liners and pleasure cruisers, and crews aboard cargo vessels and tramp steamers, crowded round the loud-speakers and radio sets to hear the Royal marriage.

Some months afterwards, the Princess and the Duke had first-hand evidence of this, when they went to London's docks to visit the New Zealand sailing ship, *Pamir*. Her master, Captain H. S. Collier, told them how, in the midst of the wastes of the South Atlantic, he and his wife and all his ship's company had listened to every word of the wedding, as it took place several thousand miles away. He showed them the ship's chart, with a pin-point marking of the exact spot where the *Pamir* hove-to, hundreds of miles from the nearest land, to give all the crew a chance to listen.

Though more people thus took part distantly in the wedding, the number of guests within the grey ancient walls of Westminster Abbey itself was by contrast smaller than at any similar occasion of State for many years. This was because the iron shadow of austerity fell athwart even this happiest of Royal days. Neither labour nor materials could be spared to build special stands, inside the Abbey or out, with the result that instead of the 10,000 guests who were accommodated within the Abbey for the Coronation, seats were available for only 2,250. The same considerations prevented the erection of stands along the route, which caused the price of window seats overlooking the Royal procession to rise to ten guineas a head. But the crowds turned out just the same, careless of the absence of stands, undaunted by the fact that the King, on Cabinet advice, had refrained from proclaiming the day as a public holiday, save for the schoolchildren: determined to cheer, even if they could not all see, their much-loved Princess on her bridal day. So great, indeed, were the crowds, that a total of 5,700 police were on duty to control them—more than twice the number of wedding guests.

Princess Elizabeth, like many another happy bride, was up betimes on her wedding morning. In her own rooms on the second floor of Buckingham Palace, tended by the faithful Margaret MacDonald, with experts from the dressmakers standing by to help, the Princess donned her lovely wedding gown, while her eight bridesmaids, the traditional number for a Royal bride, fluttered round the red-carpeted corridors of the Palace like so many spirits of beauty in their long dresses of ivory satin and net silk tulle, embroidered with syringa flowers, with wreaths of white flowers in their hair, white bouquets of lilies and orchids held in their white-gloved hands, waiting. At the head of the bride's retinue were two Princesses, her sister Margaret, aged seventeen, and her cousin Alexandra of Kent, not quite eleven, and youngest of the eight. The others were the Hon. Margaret Elphinstone, aged twenty-two, and a cousin of the bride; Miss Diana Bowes-Lyon, aged twenty-four, and also a cousin; Lady Caroline Montagu-Douglas-Scott, twenty-year-old daughter of the Duke and Duchess of Buccleuch; twenty-three-year-old Lady Mary Cambridge, another cousin, who had been a bridesmaid with Princess Elizabeth at the weddings of the Duke and Duchess of Kent and the Duke and Duchess of Gloucester; twenty-three-year-old Lady Elizabeth Lambart, daughter of the Earl and Countess of Cavan, and a close friend of the Princess's; and Lady Pamela Mountbatten, daughter of the Earl and Countess Mountbatten. Princess Elizabeth had two pages to carry her train, her two young cousins, Prince William of Gloucester, aged nearly six, and Prince Michael of Kent, a few months younger, who were dressed alike in white satin shirts, with lace jabots, and kilts of Royal Stuart tartan.

Long before she was due to leave the Princess was ready, her pearl and diamond tiara, lent by the Queen, holding her veil securely in place after a certain amount of preliminary trouble, her eyes aglow with happy excitement, her whole being radiant with joy, as she walked through the long corridors, where Palace officials and Royal servants gave her respectful greeting, to show herself in bridal array to her father and mother.

On her wedding day, as on every other day of her life, Princess Elizabeth wore a bracelet of platinum, the story of which has never been told. It is of graduated cubes of the precious metal, the centre cube containing one of the smallest watches in the world. The bracelet was a present to the Princess from Monsieur Lebrun, President of the French Republic, in commemoration of the State visit by the King and Queen to France in 1938, and she has worn it constantly ever since.

Meanwhile, over at Kensington Palace, where he had stayed the night with his mother, Princess Alice, "His Royal Highness the Bridegroom" was also preparing for the ceremony, with the aid of his cousin and fellow officer of the Royal Navy, Lieutenant the Marquess of Milford Haven, as his best man.

It was only the night before that his father-in-law-to-be had bestowed his Dukedom,

The engagement picture. At Buckingham Palace after the official announcement, the Princess and Lieutenant Mountbatten smile happily together. This was the first picture showing the Princess's engagement ring.

Their secret out. Princess Elizabeth and her fiancé, Lieut. Philip Mountbatten, together for the first time on the balcony of Buckingham Palace.

together with the rank style and title of a Royal Highness and a Prince, on the erstwhile Lieutenant Philip Mountbatten. The official documents, even the elaborate printed ceremonial issued by the Lord Chamberlain himself, contained no reference to him as a Duke or Prince, for the secret of his new title had been well-kept.

The new Duke put on his naval uniform, with the ordinary short service jacket and flat peaked cap, for his wedding. The more elaborate full-dress uniform of peace-time, with its frock coat and cocked hat, had been ruled out by the King as out of keeping with the shortages of the time. But since it was an occasion of State, as well as one of great personal import to himself, he wore the Star of the Order of the Garter and a second Star, that of the Greek Order of the Redeemer which, as a member of the Greek Royal family, he received at birth. Like other young naval officers of to-day, the Duke had no sword of his own. On his wedding day he wore the sword worn by his grandfather, Admiral Prince Louis of Battenberg, the famous First Sea Lord who did so much to prepare the Royal Navy for the war of 1914-18.

It is typical of the easy manner which helps to endear the Duke of Edinburgh to so many people of widely differing rank, that in the midst of the bustle of preparation on his wedding morning, he could think of others. Outside Kensington Palace, a group of reporters stood waiting in the chill of the November morning. When the Duke and his cousin went out to take the air for a moment or two, the Duke noticed the newspapermen and women, crossed over for a talk with them, and invited them inside for a cup of coffee. That was a Royal act which won the bridegroom a real place in the hearts of the reporters, just as, on his wedding eve, he had gladdened the hearts of half a dozen Press photographers, waiting at the Dorchester Hotel, where he gave his pre-wedding bachelor party, by asking them in, letting them take several pictures, and then, with his guests, borrowing their cameras to take some photographs themselves.

From Kensington Palace, the Duke and his best man went in a Royal car, which the King had sent over from the Royal Mews, to the Abbey. They passed along the processional route, down Constitution Hill, along the Mall, and across to the Abbey, escorted by a posse of motor-cycle police. As the patient crowds, most of whom had been in position since the very early morning, caught sight of the bridegroom, they cheered and waved and called "Good luck, Philip" in the good-humoured, friendly way that London crowds have. The bridegroom was delighted at his welcome. He smiled back at the

crowds, leaned forward to wave at them, as happy a bridegroom as has ever made his way to the altar.

Already, within the Abbey, the guests sat waiting, while the sub-organist, Dr. Osborne Peasgood, played Elgar's *Sonata in G Major*, Widor's *Andante Cantabile*, Bach's *Fugue Alla Giga*, and Bach's *Jesu, Joy of Man's Desiring*, all of them, like the rest of the music at the service, chosen by the Princess herself. Under the soft radiance of the Abbey lights, with the thin November sunshine patterning the walls with pastel colours through the stained-glass windows, the great congregation sat expectant. Ministers of the Crown, Peers and Members of Parliament (so limited was the seating that the M.P.s had to ballot for their places), representatives of each of the Dominions, including Field Marshals, Ambassadors and Ministers, Admirals, Generals and Air Marshals, were there with their womenfolk. So, too, were less important folk, N.C.O.s of the Princess's own regiments, naval ratings who had served with the Duke, members of the domestic staff from the Palace and from the Mountbatten home, girls who had made her wedding gown, and other humble folk connected with one or other of the organisations in which the bride and groom are interested. They sat there, a representative gathering of Britons and others, invited to witness a great moment in the Empire story: and the black morning coats, the dull khaki and Service blue uniforms, the grey and blue lounge suits of the men guests, the plainly-cut day dresses of the women, the absence of tiaras, while robbing the scene of much of the magnificence of Royal weddings of earlier and fuller days, gave the setting a fitting touch of reality that was in harmony with the high-minded seriousness of purpose which characterises both the Princess and her husband. Only the scarlet tunics and high white plumed helmets of the Gentlemen-at-Arms, the scarlet and gold uniforms of the Yeomen of the Guard, and the red uniforms of the Military Knights of Windsor, on duty in the Lanterns and the Choir, the Nave, and outside the Chapel of St. George, gave a touch of colour to the scene.

Soon, at the great West Door a glittering group arrived, the foreign Kings and Queens, Princes and Princesses, all of them relatives or close personal friends of the bride and bridegroom, who had come to grace the occasion with their presence. The tall King of Norway, great-uncle of the bride; young King Michael of Roumania, himself newly fallen in love with another wedding guest, Princess Anne of Bourbon-Parma; the smiling King of Denmark, his massive frame towering over his small wife; the Queen of Greece; Queen Helen of Roumania; King Peter and Queen Alexandra of Jugo-Slavia; Queen Victoria Eugénie of Spain; Queen Marie of Jugo-Slavia; Prince Charles of Belgium; Princess Juliana and Prince Bernhard of the Netherlands; the Crown Prince and Princess of Sweden; Prince and Princess George of Greece; the Duchess of Aosta; Princess Christopher of Greece; Princess Eugénie of Greece; Princess Axel of Denmark; Prince and Princess Réné of Bourbon-Parma; Prince George of Denmark; Prince Fleming of Denmark; Prince John of Luxembourg and Princess Elizabeth of Luxembourg, waited with members of our own Royal family, and the bridegroom's mother, Princess Andrew of Greece.

Unseen by the vast majority of the Abbey guests, the bridegroom entered with his best man through the Poets Corner door, and walked to his seat at the South Side of the Sacrarium steps. He looked calm and self-possessed, exchanging whispered comments with his cousin.

QUEEN OF TO-MORROW

The bridegroom arrives: the Duke's hand is on his sword, while his best man holds his high.

From the West Door, where they were met by the Dean and Chapter of Westminster, the Queen, a magnificent figure in a dress composed entirely of gold and apricot lamé, with the broad ribbon of the Garter in striking contrast across her corsage, with Queen Mary, also regal and magnificent in a dress and flowing hip-length cape of aquamarine-coloured chenille velvet, with a high collar of pearls and a necklace of gleaming diamonds, and the Garter ribbon also across her corsage, walked in slow procession up the aisle, preceded by some of the foreign Royal guests, and followed by the Kings of Norway and Denmark, and the Queens of Denmark and Greece. The bridegroom's mother walked with the Queen and Queen Mary, and the great company in the Abbey bowed and curtsied as they passed to their places in the Sacrarium to the soft cadences of Handel's *Water Music*. The Queen showed no emotion. Her gaze was as calm, her smile as unruffled, as ever, but her thoughts must have been far away, across St. James's Park, at Buckingham Palace, where, at that moment, precisely at sixteen minutes past eleven, her dearly-loved daughter was setting out on the most important journey of her life.

Under the glass portico at the Grand Entrance to Buckingham Palace, the Irish Coach stood waiting. Through the double glass doors and down the red-carpeted steps came the Princess, her hand on her father's arm, her face mantled with unusual colour. The King, in naval uniform, handed his daughter into the carriage, helped her to arrange her billowing train. As the bridal coach, with its escort of the Household Cavalry, swept out of the great iron gates of the Palace, the crowd, packed into every inch of space round the Victoria Memorial, thundered a welcoming cheer, which lasted the whole way to the distant Abbey. Gay and splendid in their uniforms of blue and scarlet, their polished breastplates gleaming, their white and red plumed helmets nodding, the Life Guards and Horse Guards rode in front and behind the Princess's coach, proud, as always, to be guarding the King and his daughter, even a little prouder, too, on this occasion, to be appearing again for the first time since before the war in the proper panoply of their full-dress uniforms.

The Princess bowed and waved her responses to the tremendous greeting of the crowds, the pearls and crystals of her dress gleaming many-coloured in the morning light as she leaned forward. At her side, the King sat erect and almost motionless, content, after once saluting in acknowledgement of the cheers as the procession left the Palace, to leave the cheering and the applause to her. After that, it was Princess Elizabeth's day,

The King takes his daughter to the Abbey. In the Irish State Coach, Princess Elizabeth leaves Buckingham Palace for the last time as an unmarried girl.

The smiling bride: Princess Elizabeth looks out at the crowds on her way to the Abbey.

and her father sat back. The blue and yellow banners initialled "E" and "P" flew from the tall flagstaffs along the route, bands played lively airs, and the whole atmosphere was full of gaiety and happiness.

Punctual to the minute, the bride arrived at the Abbey at twenty-eight minutes past eleven. Lining the way to the West Door, where the Dean and Chapter awaited her, was the guard of honour of men of her own regiments, the Grenadier Guards, the 16th/5th Lancers and the Argyll and Sutherland Highlanders, with a detachment of petty officers of the Royal Navy, from Corsham, where the Duke of Edinburgh had been stationed. Nor did the Princess forget the women of her own service, the A.T.S. Eight girls in khaki, chosen from the whole of the Service, stood as smart and trim as any of the Guardsmen.

The notes of Parry's *Bridal March* died away, the high, stirring silver notes of a fanfare played by the trumpeters of the Royal School of Music filled the morning air with gladness, proclaiming that the bride had arrived. Every head in the packed nave turned as the bridal procession began the slow walk up the crimson carpeted centre aisle to the distant Sacrarium, gleaming golden under the radiance of clusters of lamps and the softer glow of the tall candles flanking the altar. Following the fanfare, one of three composed specially for the Princess's wedding by the Master of the King's Musick, Sir Arnold Bax, came the lovely cadence of the triple choir, the Gentlemen and Children of the Chapel Royal, and the choir of St. George's Windsor, joined with the Abbey choir, singing the hymn, "Praise, My Soul, the King of Heaven", which the Princess had herself chosen as the introductory hymn. It is one of her own favourite hymns, and was sung at the wedding of the King and Queen. By a minor coincidence, the Royal wedding day marked the centenary of its author, the Rev. H. F. Lyte, whose best-known hymn is "Abide With Me".

Princess Elizabeth walked through the church with apparent assured confidence, her left hand, half hidden under the lily-petal cuff of her long sleeve, resting lightly on her father's arm. There was little to show the excitement, perhaps the slight nervousness, that must have filled her being as she paced slowly with her father between the long rows of guests, whose bows and curtsies seemed like the ripple of summer wind on a field of corn. Though she had patiently rehearsed every part of the great ceremony and service the night before in the Abbey with the King and Queen, the vivid brightness of the concealed ciné-lamps, the crowded congregation, the fresh memory of the great reception she had just received from the crowds outside, all added to the natural tension

Her father looks on solicitously as Princess Elizabeth prepares to enter the Abbey.

165

which possesses any bride on her wedding day. But Princess Elizabeth kept these feelings under strict control. Only a heightened colour in her cheek, a brighter sparkle in her eye, hinted at them to those who knew her well.

At last the long walk came to its end at the Sacrarium steps, where her bridegroom stood awaiting her.

The echoes of the singing lost themselves in the high-vaulted Abbey roof, and the voice of the Dean of Westminster, Dr. Alan C. Don, began to intone the familiar words of the Introduction to the Marriage Service, "Dearly beloved, we are gathered in the sight of God and in the face of this congregation to join together this man and this woman in holy matrimony . . ." By the King's orders, the service was planned on the same lines as previous Royal weddings. But though the bride and groom were of Royal rank, though the occasion was one of great ceremony, of constitutional and historic importance, the order of service was the same, the vows taken by the Princess and the Duke were identical, as the Archbishop of York was to remind them in his address, with those of any other couple of high rank or low, marrying according to the rites of the Church of England.

Like the great Queen Victoria, great-great-grandmother of both herself and her bridegroom, Princess Elizabeth vowed, as a woman, to obey her husband. The inclusion of the word "obey" in the Princess's marriage vows gave offence to some of the extreme advocates for sex equality. But what these extremists overlooked was that according to the strict letter of the law there was no alternative, even had the Princess desired, as there is nothing to show she did, to omit the word. The new form of service in the Revised Prayer Book, though permissive, is not yet part of the law of the land, for Parliament has never approved the new Book, and, legal though all marriages solemnised in the new form certainly are, in the case of the Heiress of Britain, the use of a form of service still awaiting Parliamentary sanction would scarcely have been fitting.

Four clergy took part in the wedding service: the Archbishop of Canterbury, Dr. Geoffrey Fisher; the Archbishop of York, Dr. Cyril Garbett; the Dean of Westminster, Dr. Don; and the Precentor of Westminster, the Rev. Cyril Armitage. The Bishop of London, Dean of His Majesty's Chapels Royal, the Bishop of Norwich, Clerk of the Closet, and the Moderator of the General Assembly of the Church of Scotland (in tribute to the fact that the Princess's inheritance is of both Kingdoms) were also present, but took no active part.

It was the Archbishop of Canterbury, as Primate of All England, and spiritual Head of the Established Church, who solemnised the wedding of the King's elder daughter. As he stood, arrayed in his full white and gold robes of State, his gorgeous cope and high mitre, administering their marriage vows to the Royal pair standing just below him on the Sacrarium steps, as the voices of the bridegroom and bride, first the deep, firm tones of Philip, then the lighter, softer tones of Elizabeth, uttered the simple well-known words of troth that bound them man and wife, there was as deep a feeling of emotion, as wishful a prayer for the happiness of the young couple with so splendid and so weighty a future before them, as ever the old Abbey in all its long nine centuries of history has known.

The King, standing on his daughter's left, seemed pensive, and a little solitary, as fathers are apt to do on such occasions. The Queen, too, from her place on the left of the Archbishop, watched the scene with a full heart, recalling, perhaps, that April day nearly twenty-five years before, when she had stood in that same place, a bride herself, marrying the King's son. On the other side of the Sacrarium, the bridegroom's mother, Princess Andrew of Greece, watched her son with love and pride. Further to her left, her brother, Rear-Admiral Earl Mountbatten of Burma, sometime guardian to the bridegroom, and still his most admired exemplar, looked on, his own wife lovely in white next to him. Tall columns of white flowers flanked the High Altar, on which was set out the wonderful gold plate of the Abbey.

From his cousin, Lord Milford Haven, the Duke of Edinburgh took the wedding ring, a plain circle of gold made from the same nugget from a Welsh mine as was that of the Queen, received it again from the Archbishop, and placed it with loving care on the finger of his bride. He and the Princess knelt, while the Archbishop pronounced them man and wife, and gave the final blessing. The newly married pair moved forward, attended only by Princess Margaret and the two pages, to the High Altar, as the joyful voices of the choir lifted again in the words of the sixty-seventh Psalm, "God be merciful to us and bless us . . ."

After the Lesser Litany, and prayers by the Precentor and the Dean, a traditional feature of Royal weddings, one of the few items differentiating this from other marriage services, followed. It was the singing by the choir of a Motet, a short passage from the Scriptures, chosen by the Precentor and set to music by the Organist of the Abbey as one of his regular duties on great Royal occasions. For this wedding, Dr. William McKie composed a most appropriate setting for the words: "We wait for thy loving kindness, O God . . ."

It was in his address, delivered to the Royal couple kneeling at the High Altar, that the

Within the Abbey. The Princess on her father's arm, followed by her bridal retinue, walks slowly up the aisle.

167

Robed in his vestments, and mitred, the Archbishop of Canterbury conducts the marriage service. The King stands on his daughter's left, to give her away. On the left are the Earl and Countess Mountbatten, who flew home from India for the wedding.

Archbishop of York put the Royal wedding in its true and absolute perspective. "One of you, the daughter of our much loved King and Queen, has already gained the affection of all. The other, as a sailor, has a sure place in the hearts of a people who know how much they owe to the strong shield of the Royal Navy," said the Archbishop. "Notwithstanding its splendour and national significance, the service in this abbey is, in all essentials, exactly the same as it would be for any cottager who might be married this afternoon in some small country church in a remote village in the Dales. The same vows are taken: the same prayers offered: and the same blessings are given.

"Never before has a wedding been followed with so much interest by so many, and this interest has not been merely passive; it has been accompanied by the heartfelt prayers and good wishes of millions, and the hope that throughout your married life you may have every happiness and joy."

The wedding service was, as was right and proper for the future Queen of England, according to the Church of England: and perhaps among the more fervid of Scots there may have been some feeling that, since the bride was equally their own future Queen as well, some claim could be made for a Scottish element in the service. If that were the case, the Princess, albeit unconsciously, showed her inherent gift of statesmanship by her choice of the hymn to follow the Archbishop's address. It was Psalm 23 which the Princess chose, the Scottish metrical version of the psalm, "The Lord's my Shepherd, I'll not want", sung, as she has so often heard it sung on Deeside and in Edinburgh, to the tune "Crimond". The real reason for her choice was the plain, personal one that she likes the hymn sung in this manner: but the fact that a Scottish hymn was sung at the Royal wedding gave great satisfaction to thousands of simple Scottish hearts.

Amid all this solemnity, amid the splendid pageantry of State, where all went with clockwork precision and smoothness, it was left to the Princess's two small pages to supply the human touch. Carrying the fifteen-feet pearl-encrusted bridal train was a difficult task for the two five-year-olds, even though they had rehearsed their duties several times. As the bride moved up the steps towards the altar, the train caught in the base of a tall candlestick, defying the efforts of Prince Michael and Prince William to free it. The King himself bent down to aid them before it came away. Again, as the party moved away to the Chapel of St. Edward the Confessor for the signing of the register, Prince Michael caught his foot, tripped and fell. But he was up again in a moment, and after that there was no further trouble.

Orlando Gibbons' lovely threefold "Amen" brought the service to an end, a second fanfare of trumpets soared through the still air, and everyone joined in the National Anthem.

In the hallowed sanctuary of the Edward the Confessor Chapel, where six Kings and three Queens of England have their last resting place, the Duke and his new Duchess, the King and Queen, Queen Mary, and many other members of the Royal family, signed the marriage registers. As with all Royal weddings, four separate registers were signed, including the special Royal register and the Abbey's own ivory-covered record of Royal marriages. Wesley's anthem, "Blessed be the God and Father", with the treble solo, "Love one another with a pure heart fervently", which was sung at the christening of Princess Elizabeth, was sung by the triple choir while the congregation waited. The third and last silver trumpet fanfare heralded their appearance, followed

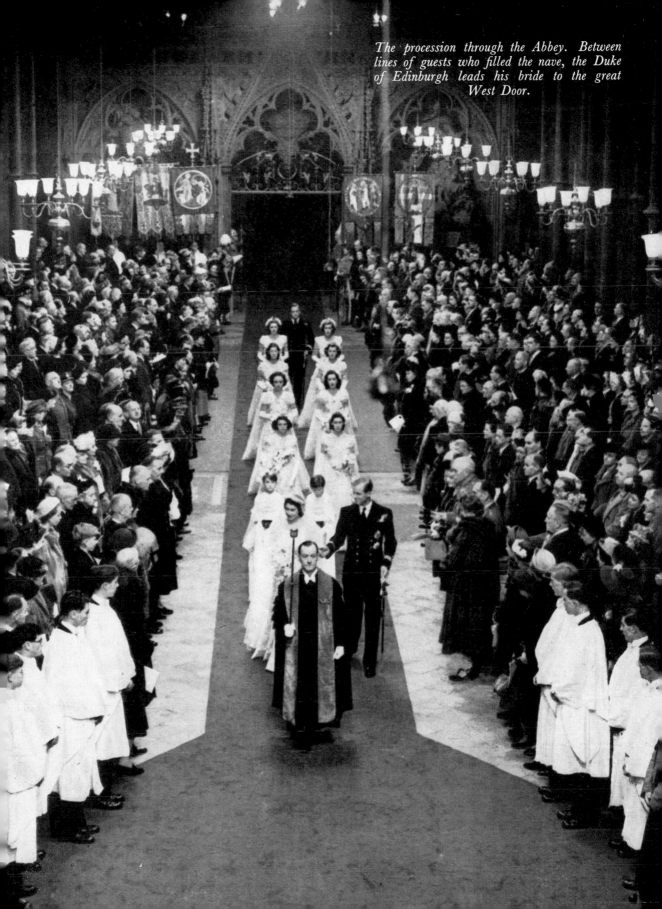

The procession through the Abbey. Between lines of guests who filled the nave, the Duke of Edinburgh leads his bride to the great West Door.

Man and wife. This happy, unposed picture taken as the Princess and the Duke appeared outside the Abbey is the one which Princess Elizabeth likes the most.

by the familiar notes of Mendelssohn's *Wedding March*. Her veil thrown back, her face radiant with new-found happiness, Princess Elizabeth, Duchess of Edinburgh, walked again in procession down the aisle, preceded by the Dean and the dignitaries of the Abbey, followed by her pages and her bridesmaids, but this time with her left hand held lightly in her husband's right. Once more, curtsies and bows swept through the crowded nave, heads were turned, this time to follow the bride and groom to the open West Door, outside which, in the raw November chill, thousands waited to acclaim the Princess on the happiest day of her life. As she paused at her husband's side, before they entered the fairy-tale Glass Coach to drive back to Buckingham Palace, she waved her hand to the cheering crowds in the gesture of acknowledgement that she has made her own, while scores of photographers recorded the scene. The route to the Palace was along the same roads over which she had driven so short a time before with her father, but the waiting crowds were thicker than ever, their welcome to the Princess and her handsome husband even more charged with enthusiasm than it had been to the still unmarried Princess of two hours earlier.

Other Royal brides and grooms in recent years have made their way back to the Palace after the ceremony by an extended route, including St. James's Street, Piccadilly, and Hyde Park Corner. No personal choice of the Princess, but security considerations by the Cabinet, prompted doubtless by the current threats of terrorism over the Palestine question, caused the breaking of this tradition.

Outside Buckingham Palace, bigger crowds than any since the Coronation gave a great roar of welcome as the bridal coach swept through the centre gates with its attendant escort of the Household Cavalry riding before and behind. They roared again when the King and Queen returned, when the bridesmaids drove in, when the foreign Kings and Queens arrived, saving a special thunder of greeting for the beloved figure of Queen Mary, who drove with her daughter, the Princess Royal. Then the chant, "We want the bride and groom. We want Elizabeth and Philip", began. It went on without ceasing until the windows behind the crimson-and-gold draped balcony on the front of the Palace were opened, and the married pair stepped out, followed by the King and Queen, Queen Mary, Princess Andrew of Greece and other guests. The bridesmaids, the pages and the best man came out, too, filling the balcony with laughter and happiness. It was one of those occasions that London delights in, the massed throngs cheering, waving and applauding, the atmosphere of

Back to the Palace. The bride and groom in the Glass Coach.

*Now they
are married:
back from
the Abbey,
the Princess
and the
Duke appear
on the
Palace
balcony.*

*Left to right: Princess Margaret, the Hon. Margaret Elphinstone, Miss Diana Bowes
Prince William, the Bride and Bridegroom*

national rejoicing at this Royal occasion blending with the homelier feelings of family happiness: and the Princess and the Duke shared in the happiness to the full.

Neither of them made any attempt to hide their feelings as, after a final wave, they turned to re-enter the Palace. Princess Elizabeth's eyes were bright with tears of happiness; her husband, too, showed clearly that he was deeply moved. For him, more than for his bride, it has been a test, almost an ordeal, as he showed himself to the crowds for the first time as the son-in-law of the King, the husband of the future Queen. The warmth of the cheering, the repeated cries, good-natured and informal, of "Good old Philip" which mingled with the cheers, were ample proof that he had passed that test with complete success. Princess Elizabeth, like any wife lovingly sharing in her husband's success, was as delighted as the Duke himself at the ample evidence that the crowds had taken the man of her own heart to theirs.

Then came the wedding breakfast. One hundred and fifty guests sat at fifteen separate round tables, each decorated with pink carnations, in the white and gold Ball-supper Room on the first floor of the Palace. The bride and groom sat with the King and Queen, Queen Mary, and Princess Andrew of Greece at the centre table, on which, besides flowers, were sprigs of myrtle taken from a plant grown from a sprig of Queen Victoria's wedding bouquet. Under the soft light of the great rose-crystal candelabra,

Caroline Montagu-Douglas-Scott, Lady Elizabeth Lambart, the Best Man (Marquess of Milford Haven), Cambridge and Lady Pamela Mountbatten.

the gold State service glowed on the tables. But the menu, in the midst of this magnificence, was confined to the three courses dictated by austerity. All were of unrationed food. The main dish was partridge—*Perdreau en Casserole*—and, so closely had the secret of the bridegroom's new title been kept that the Royal chef, still in ignorance the night before the wedding, naming his dishes, according to custom, after the bride and groom, called his first course "Fillets de Sole Mountbatten". The third dish was "Bombe Glacée Princesse Elizabeth".

Crossing the room to where the four-tiered cake stood against the wall, the Princess and the Duke cut the first slice easily with the Duke's sword. Pieces were handed round to every guest, and the King rose to make a brief speech proposing the health of the newly married pair. His guests drank the toast in champagne from the Royal cellars, while millions of other well-wishers of the young couple, all over the world, also raised glasses to their future happiness. In accordance with the custom at Royal weddings, there were no other speeches at all.

The Princess had twelve wedding cakes, each from a well-known maker, but only one of them, the official one made at the King's order by the firm which supplied the cake for his own wedding, stood in the Ball-supper Room, on a side table in front of a wall mirror which reflected its tall white elegance. The cake weighed altogether about five hundred pounds, and stood four feet high on a silver base forty inches across. Slender silver pillars separated its four tiers, and on the top was a silver bowl containing camelias and roses. It was a white cake, as all good wedding cakes should traditionally be, but each of the four tiers bore, besides filigree canopies made of icing sugar and white figures of Cupid, coloured crests and plaques. On the bottom tier were the Princess's arms, painted on silk, with sugar plaques showing Buckingham Palace, Windsor Castle and Balmoral. On the next tier appeared the armorial bearing of the bridegroom, with plaques showing cricket and other of the Duke's pastimes. On the third tier were the crests of the Royal Navy and the Grenadier Guards, and the badge of the A.T.S., with plaques representing horse riding, swimming and other pursuits of the Princess. The top tier bore the badges of the Sea Rangers and the Girl Guides, with shields bearing the monograms of the bride and bridegroom.

The recipe used was for a normal rich wedding cake, with plenty of butter, and brandy from South Africa, rum from Jamaica, and curaçao from Trinidad added to the mixture. The cake took four months in all to make.

Conventional lucky charms, a bachelor's button, a wedding ring, a three-penny piece, a horseshoe and a donkey in silver, were in the lower tier, which the Princess and her husband cut with the Duke's sword—but there is no record of which of the guests at the wedding breakfast received them.

Small pieces of the remainder of the cake were sent later from the Palace in small white boxes bearing the initials "E.P." in silver, to hundreds of friends of the Princess and her husband, while the other eleven cakes were also cut into pieces and distributed to various hospitals and institutions with which the Princess is connected.

Before the cake cutting, there came a surprise item which the Princess had herself arranged. The doors opened, and the King's Piper, Pipe-Major A. MacDonald, late of the Scots Guards, entered, leading the four King's Pipers from Balmoral, all playing their pipes. The tunes they played, as they marched up and down among the guests, had been chosen by the Princess, who has an extensive knowledge of pipe music. The tunes were: "Dovecot Park", "The Rose among the Heather", "Jenny Dang the Weaver", and "The Green Hills of Tyrol". Each of the five pipers afterwards received a piece of wedding cake from the Princess. Outside, the crowds were calling again for the Princess and the Duke. They went to the balcony again, and the Princess, behind schedule for the first time that day, hurried off to her own apartments to change into her going-away clothes. At the Grand Entrance to the Palace, the pair-horse open landau awaited her and her husband. The King and Queen, with their guests, stood on the steps as the new husband and wife seated themselves, and the coach moved slowly off. Led by the King, the Royal and other guests, including the Queen, who hitched up her long skirt to run the better, ran across the sanded quadrangle to cut off the coach and bombard the Princess and the Duke with paper rose-petals. The King, the Queen, the best man, and some of the bridesmaids followed it to the outer gates of the Palace, treating the crowds to a rare close-up view. Then the landau disappeared down the Mall, into the gathering dusk, on its way to Waterloo Station, where the Royal honeymoon special train was waiting. The couple reached the station five minutes late and, typically, the Princess's first thought was for others. She apologised for the delay, and hoped it had not caused too much inconvenience.

ROMANCE AND MARRIAGE—THE ROYAL WEDDING

It was at Broadlands, the lovely home of Lord and Lady Mountbatten, where Lord Palmerston once lived, set in the New Forest, not far from Romsey, that the Royal pair spent the first part of their honeymoon. Quiet and peace is what all honeymoon couples desire, and in the case of the Royal couple, after all the public excitement and the crowds of their wedding day, this desire was even stronger.

Behind the walls of Broadlands, privacy was of course theirs, though the major portion of the big house was still in use, as it had been throughout the war, as a hospital. But crowds, with more curiosity than good taste, waited to stare at them every time they left the grounds. This came to its height in an unpleasant, undignified scene in ancient Romsey Abbey, where the Princess and the Duke went to attend morning service on the first Sunday of their married life. Sightseers who had come in by car and charabanc from the coast towns as well as from London, crowded into the church, craning to glimpse the Royal pair, while others, outside, clambered on the very tombstones in their irreverent eagerness to see inside. It was a deplorable exhibition, the only black spot that marred the general, nation-wide rejoicings. After a week at Broadlands, where the Duke took his wife for her first jeep ride, in a jeep belonging to his uncle, Lord Mountbatten, the Royal couple went up to Scotland for the rest of their honeymoon. The Highlands of Scotland are an unusual choice of setting for a honeymoon in December, but the Princess had always had a really deep-rooted affection for Deeside, and the country around Balmoral now had a further romantic charm for her, since it was among the mountains overlooking the King's Highland home that, it is generally agreed, the Royal couple first came to an unofficial engagement. At Birkhall, the small but comfortable house a few miles from Balmoral Castle, which the King lent them, the Princess and the Duke had a fortnight of complete privacy and unalloyed happiness. Snow fell during their stay, but from the moment the Duke took the wheel of their big limousine, H.R.H. I, outside Aberdeen Station, in the very early morning hours, to drive his bride the fifty miles to Balmoral, there was nothing to mar their holiday. A small staff, recruited from the trusted Royal servants at Balmoral, had made Birkhall—where the King and Queen used to stay, with their daughters, during the reign of King George V—ready for them, and stayed to tend their every want. At Crathie Church, where they went for service the following Sunday morning, there was no repetition of the Romsey scenes. The Marquess of Aberdeen had gone to the length of issuing a public appeal that the Royal honeymooners should be left alone and, whether as a result of this, or merely because of the inborn courtesy of the Highland folk, there certainly was no attempt at sightseeing or prying throughout their stay.

What the Royal pair themselves thought of the welcome they had received on their wedding day is best expressed in their own words, in the message to the nation which they wrote together at Buckingham Palace, where they broke their journey north from Broadlands:

"Before we leave for Scotland to-night, we want to say that the reception given us on our wedding day and the loving interest shown by our fellow-countrymen and well-wishers in all parts of the world, have left an impression which will never grow faint. We cannot find any words to express what we feel, but we can at least offer our grateful thanks to the millions who have given us this unforgettable send-off in our married life."

Just how much world interest was aroused by the Royal wedding may be judged from the one small fact that when the Princess asked to see the wedding telegrams on

The wedding photograph. The newly married Princess carries her bridal bouquet as she stands at the side of her tall sailor husband. The rich and delicate embroidery on her flowing train gleams against the background of red carpet, as it cascades over the dais steps of the Throne Room at Buckingham Palace.
Photograph by Baron.

her return to the Palace, she was shown a series of big folders, each crammed with messages, making a total of well over seven thousand!

That world interest had, of course, been growing for many months, indeed, it had been born years before, when speculation first began about whom the Princess would marry. The name of the young good-looking Prince Philip of Greece did not appear in the first lists of young men made up by the gossips: but for more than a year before the Royal engagement was officially announced in the Court Circular of July 9, 1947, friends of both the young couple were sure that their marriage was only a matter of time. The Princess kept her secret as well as she could. Official denials, with carefully worded accuracy, turned down premature newspaper reports that the Heiress to the Throne was engaged. Prince Philip, serving quietly as an instructor at the Royal Naval Training Establishment at Corsham, said nothing. But the rumours were not to be silenced. They followed the Princess to South Africa, when she went there with the King and Queen early in 1947. They grew more insistent when it was announced that Prince Philip of Greece and Denmark had

The wedding group. The Princess and her husband stand on the crimson-hung dais in the Throne Room at Buckingham Palace, with the best man, bridesmaids and pages. The King and Queen are on the Duke's left, with the Dowager Countess of Milford Haven, his grandmother. His mother, Princess Andrew, stands with Queen Mary on the Princess's right.

Send-off for the bride and groom. In the Palace courtyard best man and bridesmaids follow the honey-moon coach. Next to Lord Milford Haven is Miss Diana Bowes-Lyon, then Lady Caroline Montagu-Douglas-Scott, Lady Pamela Mountbatten and Lady Mary Cambridge.

applied for and been granted naturalisation as a British subject—a step that actually was taken by Philip independently of his marriage plans.

There were several reasons for the apparent delay in the official announcement of the engagement which, by June of 1947, had come to be an accepted fact by the great majority of people both at home and in the overseas dominions. Most important of them was the simple fact that the Princess and the future Duke were not, in fact, engaged until the very day of the announcement, since before the Princess could under-take matrimony, as one in the direct line of succession to the throne, she had to secure the formal permission of the King. Another was the need, though not a constitutional obligation, for the King to acquaint his Prime Ministers, both at home and in the Dominions, of his intentions in advance. There is nothing to require the consenting "advice" of the heads of His Majesty's governments before the marriage of the heiress to the throne, but it was with great pleasure that the King received from each of his Prime Ministers, to whom he communicated the news in advance, replies showing that the proposed match would be everywhere welcome.

Princess Elizabeth and her husband knew each other from childhood. They met with fair frequency during their childhood, for Prince Philip, though his father, the late

ROMANCE AND MARRIAGE—THE ROYAL WEDDING

Prince George of Greece, was a member of the Greek Royal House, was brought up from a very early age in this country. They met again when Philip was a Special Entry cadet at Dartmouth, preparing with great seriousness and intensity of purpose for the naval career to which he had vowed himself. This was when Princess Elizabeth went with the King and Queen on a visit to the Royal Naval College in 1939, after the King had reviewed the Reserve Fleet in Weymouth Bay under the shadow of approaching war. The young cadet and the Princess found plenty to say to each other at the College tea-party and later when Prince Philip was invited to dine with some of his brother cadets, aboard the Royal yacht.

Then came the war years. Prince Philip went proudly off to sea as a midshipman. He wrote from his ship in the Mediterranean Fleet to his cousin at Balmoral, and Princess Elizabeth answered his letters. In January, 1940, he came home on leave, full, as young men from the gunroom usually are, of the interests of life at sea and saw something of his Princess cousin. Next time leave came round, Prince Philip was invited to Windsor Castle —and they saw a good deal more of each other. By 1943, when the young Prince, now with the two rings of a lieutenant on his sleeve, again came to Windsor to stay, they were firm friends. He was one of the audience which saw the Princess and her sister in their Christmas pantomime of Aladdin, and others in the company were not slow to mark the mutual attraction of the Royal pair.

. . . and a shower of rose petals. Earl and Countess Mountbatten of Burma take a lead in the bombardment.

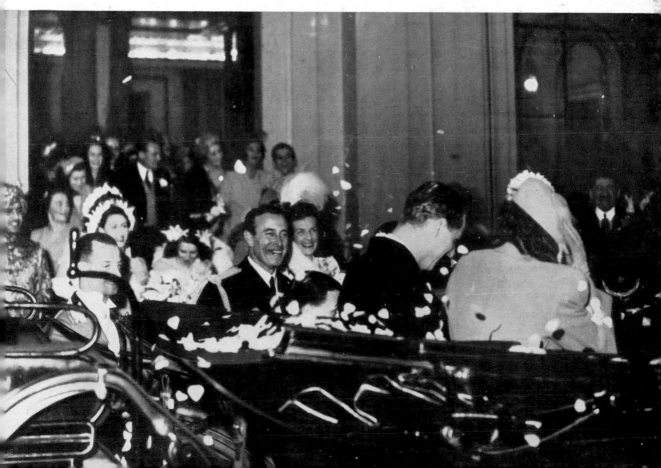

With one of the escort behind: the open landau takes the bride and groom to Waterloo Station, where their honeymoon train awaits them.

Two years passed, the war ended, and Prince Philip, while devoting himself to his naval career, kept in touch with Princess Elizabeth by letter and telephone, meeting her occasionally when he came to London on leave. In the summer of 1946, he was invited by the King to Balmoral, and the young couple spent much of their time together amid the romantic scenery of the Highlands. When Prince Philip brought down two stags on his first day's stalk, Princess Elizabeth, herself a fine shot with a sporting rifle, was the first to congratulate him. The ghillies on the King's estate who, to a man, are the willing and devoted slaves of Princess Elizabeth, sensed what was in the wind—for their craft is to be observers of nature—and were glad. Prince Philip had won their friendship for himself, and they judged him a fitting man for their much-loved Princess.

When and where the Princess and the Duke of Edinburgh became engaged has never been revealed. But it seems certain that it was during those weeks in the Highlands that their growing friendship deepened finally into love. In any case, by the time the Balmoral holiday had ended, close friends of the Royal pair had no further doubts. "It is not a question of whether the Princess and Prince Philip are engaged, but of when the engagement will be announced," declared one of them, somewhat prematurely.

ROMANCE AND MARRIAGE—THE ROYAL WEDDING

During the four months of the South African tour, the Princess smilingly parried questions, some of them much more direct than she could anticipate, about her future. "You must wait and see," she told one persistent Boer councillor who asked her if she would have "some news for us on your birthday". The birthday—her twenty-first—came and went, and there was still no news, though letters and messages went with increasing frequency between the young couple, and a telegram of greeting from Lieutenant Philip—he had now renounced his Royal titles on naturalisation—was the first to be opened by Princess Elizabeth on her birthday morning in Cape Town.

Once the Royal family was back in London, the final moves were made behind the scenes to prepare for the announcement. It says much for the discretion of statesmen in the young nations of the Commonwealth that no hint of the coming news was allowed to leak from any of the Dominion capitals, even after the cipher telegrams from Buckingham Palace giving the date of the announcement had been received. In Athens, there was a different story. No official communications, of course, passed between the Palace and the Greek authorities concerning the engagement. Lieutenant Mountbatten had severed the last tenuous ties that connected him, however slightly, with the Royal House of Greece, and as far as he was personally concerned his engagement was purely a private matter, as it is for any other subject of the King. But members of the Greek Court heard the news, as a family, rather than an official, matter, and it was from Athens that the final disclosure came the very day before the announcement was to be officially made.

Both Princess Elizabeth, and Lieutenant Mountbatten, down at Corsham, were greatly relieved when, at last, there was no longer any need for secrecy or concealment. That night, while the newspaper presses were printing the news the world had so long expected, Princess Elizabeth went to a dance at Apsley House, "Number One, London", the former home of the Iron Duke of Wellington. Lieutenant Mountbatten stayed at Corsham till the next day, when he drove himself up to the Palace in his small open sports car, to greet his fiancée and to make his first appearance on the balcony of Buckingham Palace with the King and Queen and the Princess, while a huge crowd below thundered a welcome to the young Royal lovers.

Despite all the speculation coupling his name with that of Princess Elizabeth, the former Prince of Greece was a little-known figure to the general public at the time of the engagement, and remained so even until the day of the wedding. He had lived a quiet life, away from the glare of public appearances, content to make a career for himself on his own merits in the Royal Navy. In the very

Honeymoon smiles: in the grounds of Broadlands.

democratic atmosphere of a battleship gun-room, Prince Philip earned the admiration and respect of his fellow midshipmen purely on his own personal qualities, certainly not on account of his princely rank. To-day, as a Prince of the Royal House of England, and Duke of Edinburgh, the title born by his own great-granduncle, Queen Victoria's second son, he is still anxious to be judged on his merits as a man: and, as a man of integrity, honesty, and intelligence, to say nothing of charm, he is immensely popular among all who know him. In the always delicate, sometimes even difficult, position of consort to the Heiress to the Throne, the Duke has already shown in a score of ways, not least by the candour and sincerity of his few public speeches, that he is extremely well suited for the position. Princess Elizabeth and the Duke made a love match. Of that there is no shadow of doubt. It is the good fortune of the nation and empire that the man the Princess loves is a man whom all the vast millions of her future subjects can also love and admire.

Born on June 10, 1921, at a house called Mon Repos, in the island of Corfu, where his father, Prince Andrew of Greece (who died in 1944), had gone with his English wife, Princess Alice, daughter of the Dowager Marchioness of Milford Haven, and great-granddaughter of Queen Victoria, Prince Philip was the youngest of a family of five. While still a baby, he was taken to St. Cloud, just outside Paris, where his father lived quietly away from the turmoil of Greek politics, and he has never been back to Greece since. He came to England as a small boy, and after a period at a preparatory school at Cheam, went on to a small public school run on modern lines at Gordonstoun, in Scotland. Thence, he went to the Royal Naval College at Dartmouth, where he quickly achieved the early success that has so often been the foundation of the successful naval career on which he had set his boyish ambitions. When the young Royal cadet won the King's Dirk and the Eardley-Howard-Crockett prize as the best all-round cadet, the future vision of the one broad and three thinner rings of an Admiral must have seemed very real to him. Like so many other men of his generation, he saw active service at a very early age, acquitting himself so well in the turmoil of the night battle of Cape Matapan that he was mentioned in dispatches for his coolness and efficiency as mid-shipman of the searchlight control. With this background, promotion came rapidly, and at twenty-one he found himself First Lieutenant of the destroyer H.M.S. *Whelp*, the youngest officer in the Service to hold such a post—and the Royal Navy does not make such appointments on the basis of social rank or position. Love of the Navy remains to-day one of the Duke of Edinburgh's most deeply ingrained qualities. With level-headed realism, he has accepted the fact that, as Consort of the future Queen, he can no longer envisage the kind of active career in the Service which he had intended. But until his State duties call him away, he is determined, with the full approval of the King, to continue, with all the energy and enthusiasm in his power, to work as a naval officer. At the Admiralty, where he was posted to the Operations Division for a short spell soon after the wedding, he won high esteem for his ability to estimate a situation and to take action upon it. Afterwards, at the R.N. Staff College he worked hard and conscientiously, refusing all day-time public and social engagements during term.

When he was a small boy, his uncle, the late Marquess of Milford Haven, was appointed his guardian. After his death in 1938, Lord Louis Mountbatten—now Earl Mountbatten of Burma—took over the duties of guardianship, and to-day "Uncle

The Princess and the Duke look at some of their wedding pictures: a happy informal photograph at Broadlands, where they spent the first part of their honeymoon.

Dickie", as Lord Mountbatten is known, stands almost in the relationship of father to the Duke.

Fair-haired, tall, good-looking, the Duke of Edinburgh, thoroughly English by upbringing, has that intense love of England and the British way of life, that deep devotion to the ideals of peace and liberty for which Britain stands, that are characteristic of so many naval men. To the King, himself a naval man, it was an added pleasure that the man of his daughter's choice should, in addition to all his other qualities, come from the Senior Service, which the King regards as one of the finest training grounds for men in the whole world.

The Duke and his wife have a common ancestor in Queen Victoria, their great-great-grandmother. Before he took his mother's family name, Mountbatten, on his naturalisation, the Duke, as Prince Philip, had no surname. His family, the House of Schleswig-Holstein-Sonderburg-Glucksburg, followed the very ancient Royal custom of using no patronymic.

It was on February 28, 1947, that Prince Philip, paying the ordinary fees of £10 2s. 6d., became a British subject, as a serving officer, by naturalisation, fulfilling a purpose that had been his since before the outbreak of war. Five months later, on July 31, 1947, he was one of the two central, though not personally present, figures, in an act of constitutional and historic importance, when the King at Buckingham Palace held a Privy Council, summoned for the express purpose of declaring the Assent of the Sovereign in Council to the marriage of his daughter with Lieutenant Philip Mountbatten. This Council, prescribed by the Royal Marriages Act of 1772 as an essential preliminary before marriage for all the descendants of King George II who have not attained the age of twenty-five, was attended by more than the usual four Privy Councillors, which enabled His Majesty's Loyal Opposition, as well as the Dominions, to be represented. Those attending the brief but momentous meeting were: the Duke of Gloucester, the Archbishop of Canterbury, the Lord Chancellor (Lord Jowitt), the Prime Minister (Mr. Attlee), the Lord President of the Council (Mr. Herbert Morrison), the Secretary of State for Commonwealth Relations (Viscount Addison), the Home Secretary (Mr. Chuter Ede), the Leader of the Opposition (Mr. Winston Churchill), Mr. C. D. Howe (Minister of Reconstruction and Supply, Canada), Mr. J. A. Beasley (High Commissioner for Australia), Mr. W. J. Jordan (High Commissioner for New Zealand), Mr. James Stratford (former Chief Justice of South Africa), and Sir Alan Lascelles (Private Secretary to the King).

After the Council, at which the King declared his formal consent to the coming marriage, under the Great Seal of the Realm, he sent telegrams to the Governors-General, his personal representatives in the four Dominions, asking them to communicate his action to their respective councils—the Privy Council for Canada, and the Executive Councils of the other three Dominions.

That was the last formality to be observed. Now the way lay clear for the love-match of the Princess, heiress to the greatest throne in the world, and the man of her choice, then a plain Lieutenant in the Royal Navy, without Royal rank or precedence.

CHAPTER TWELVE

What To-morrow May Bring: The Princess's Future

WHEN Mr. Winston Churchill, some forty-odd years ago, made a winning bet that the British Empire would last another ten years, even that sagacious, far-sighted statesman had little conception of the kind of Empire which to-day is the proud and mighty future inheritance that faces Princess Elizabeth. Nor could her grandfather, whose last words as he lay on his death-bed at Sandringham House on a bleak day of January 1936 were "How is the Empire?" foresee the great constitutional changes, the formation of new Dominions, the abolition of the Indian Empire, with its consequent change in the Royal titles, that have come about in the last few years. From her inside position at the centre of imperial affairs, Princess Elizabeth, who learned so much about the evolution of our Commonwealth in her schooldays, has seen the very shape of the Empire, over which she will one day be called upon to rule, in the process of dynamic change. Her own future, as Heiress Presumptive, is inextricably bound up with the future of the Empire; nor is it too much to say that the future of the Empire is also bound with that of the Princess. She has already given overwhelming proof of the serious purpose with which she regards that destiny, and her own great personal triumph during the South African tour, which at the same time gave her her first sight of the overseas Dominions, and the people of the overseas Empire their first sight of their future Queen, is an augury of the happiest kind for the relationships of the Crown with its subjects in the great Dominions to-morrow. The people of Australia and New Zealand would have been delighted had the Princess and her husband been able to take part in the Royal tour planned for 1949. This was not possible. But visits to Canada, Australia, and New Zealand, perhaps to India, Pakistan and Ceylon, are certainly among the most important of the undertakings in the as yet unwritten diary of the Princess's future.

That the Empire wants to see Princess Elizabeth is certain. That Princess Elizabeth wants to see the Empire is equally sure. She has made no secret of her wishes in this direction, and her father, who has found his own wide travel and personal knowledge of his Dominions of such immense value in his duties as Sovereign, is naturally anxious that his daughter should enjoy the same advantages as part of her training for the Throne. Up to now, no real opportunity has presented itself for a further Empire visit since the Princess returned with her parents from South Africa. Not many weeks after that, she was immersed in the welter of preparations for her forthcoming wedding. In some parts of the Empire, notably in Canada, there was a feeling that the Princess and her husband might have spent part at least of their honeymoon in one of the Dominions, but this was not possible for a variety of reasons, chief among which was the understandable desire of the young Royal couple to spend their honeymoon as a honeymoon, that is to say in complete privacy, without any of the necessity for official functions or receptions which would have inevitably had to take place during any Dominion visit. Time, too, was a factor, for the Royal honeymoon lasted under four weeks, scarcely long enough a period for an Empire visit by the Heiress Presumptive and her Consort. In any case, it would be contrary to Princess Elizabeth's sense of what is fitting for her to make her first visit to one of her father's great Dominions purely as a short holiday trip. When she goes to Canada, or any other part of the Empire, she will want to go among the people, to visit the great cities, to see the centres of production and industry, the Parliaments and the seats of government, so that she may return home with a real and full understanding of the country, its people, and their problems.

All such tours are questions very much of the future, for the Princess has a natural wish to remain at home in her own new family circle for the next year or two. In this, as in nearly everything, she has the full support of her parents. The King and Queen both know the sadness entailed on parents who have to leave a small baby behind while they go on a six months' tour of Empire. This is what they themselves had to do when Princess Elizabeth was a baby of nine months. Immediately after their own wedding, the King and Queen were involved in such a spate of public engagements that, as the King afterwards was wont to remark, "We scarcely had time to see each other". He determined that a like fate should not overtake his daughter and her husband nearly twenty-five years later, which is why so many requests for attendance by the Princess and the Duke of Edinburgh were firmly rejected in the first months of their married life. It is logical to conclude that similar feelings will cause the King to regard with little favour any submissions from his Empire Prime Ministers for a visit by the Princess and her husband for many many months to come, certainly as far ahead as 1950.

When the Princess does go overseas, Canada, as the senior Dominion, would appear to have the prior claim. A Canadian visit, too, would have the advantage of affording an opportunity for the President and people of the United States to invite the Princess and the Duke to visit them—an opportunity which they are likely to embrace with great eagerness, to judge from the constant and affectionate cousinly interest which Americans of all classes display in her life and activities.

Constitutionally, there is no impediment to stop Princess Elizabeth or her husband, the Duke of Edinburgh, being appointed Governor-General of one of the Dominions. A recommendation to this effect from one of the King's Governments would undoubtedly receive most careful and prolonged consideration, because of the possible complications which might, in certain eventualities, ensue. The Duke of Edinburgh is first and foremost a serving naval officer and any visits that they may carry out will largely depend on the nature of the Duke's duties, at any rate in the immediate future.

Meanwhile, at home, the Princess's immediate future is bounded by the happy frontiers of family life. Herself the daughter of a happy home, she views the future of her own family happiness with every anticipation of delight, for she knows that the deepest roots of human joy, for Princess or commoner, lie in the family circle.

Her marriage and the foundation of a family life of her own have naturally withdrawn the Princess from the immediate circle of her father and mother and sister. Princess Elizabeth and Princess Margaret are not quite so much together as they used to be in the Princess's single days when they were sometimes known as the "Royal Inseparables". But marriage has done nothing to lessen the deep affection between the Royal sisters, and though the Princesses no longer appear together so often on public occasions, in private they see much of each other and spend a great deal of time together. This was particularly the case while Princess Elizabeth was living at Buckingham Palace and the Duke of Edinburgh was away at Greenwich taking the course at the Royal Naval Staff College.

Princess Elizabeth and her husband, like the King and Queen, are firm believers in the British tradition of the country week-end. There is nothing that gives them more pleasure than a quiet Saturday and Sunday at Windlesham Moor, their home at Sunningdale, with no public engagements or official functions to interfere with their private relaxation. The Duke, who is a lover of outdoor sport, particularly of cricket, runs a team of his own, playing on Sundays on the delightful private Royal cricket ground not far from the Long Walk in Windsor Great Park. Like other wives of cricket enthusiasts, Princess Elizabeth goes over with her husband to watch the play, and when the match is over, she likes, as the captain's wife, to invite some of the players, if not all of them, back to Windlesham for a cup of tea or a drink. Often, the King strolls down from Royal Lodge to watch the play, and afterwards he will look in at the little informal party at Windlesham, taking great delight in the happiness of his daughter and son-in-law. Members of the Princess's and the Duke's Household, fellow students from Greenwich, Service friends and others play for the Duke's team, and though the standard of play may not be quite up to the requirements of Lord's, the true spirit of English country cricket imbues these friendly Royal games.

But delightful and attractive as these simple pleasures of domesticity and family life may be, they form only the background of the Princess's life, albeit a background without which she would be nothing like so well equipped for the great duties which are hers. Her family circle is the family circle of the Empire, the prototype of all the millions of families all over the globe who add up into the family of the British Commonwealth of Nations. It is the good fortune of that Commonwealth to have as happy a family in the younger generation of the Royal family as in the older. Millions of people share vicariously in the happiness of Princess Elizabeth. Details of her private life would naturally be of the greatest interest to them, but there is a general measure of agreement throughout the Empire that she is well entitled to what she herself claims, the right to some privacy and freedom from intrusion. This side of her life Princess Elizabeth guards with some care. There is little more calculated to make her really angry than unwarranted attempts to pry into her private concerns. Her public life she devotes freely, with all the enthusiasm and strength of her generous nature, to the peoples of her father's Kingdoms: her private life she regards as her own, a division with which none can wish to quarrel, especially when the relative proportions of time which she gives to public and private affairs respectively are considered.

Thus it is the public side of the Princess's life which is of the greater importance and concern to the outside world. In the months during which she has been undertaking no public engagements in preparation for the birth of her baby this autumn, the absence of her familiar, smiling smile, the lack of reports of her activities and speeches has brought real regret to hundreds of thousands of her devoted admirers, for her forthright personality,

Another Royal Wedding group on the Palace balcony: after the Silver Wedding service of their Majesties the King and Queen. Left to right: the Duke of Edinburgh, Princess Elizabeth, the Duke and Duchess of Gloucester, the Queen, the King, Princess Margaret and Queen Mary.

her spontaneous kindness, her sympathy for the unfortunate, in a world that is sadly out of date, her goodness, have given her an unchallengeable place in the affections of the world. She is the acknowledged leader and spokesman of British youth, a position which she has won for herself by her actions and words in the few years since she first made her full entry upon the public scene, and one which she regards as the greatest of her present responsibilities. No cause is nearer her heart than the cause of youth, no call more important to her than the call for opportunity for the young, especially for the men and women of her own generation whose early lives were shadowed so deeply by war. When she resumes her active part in public life, she will continue to give pride of place to engagements connected with the welfare of young folk, and to work in every way that lies in her power to improve the lot of the young citizens of to-day and to-morrow. Even while she has been unable to appear in person at meetings, the Princess has not relinquished her interest in the activities of the many youth organisations with which she is connected, reading reports, studying future plans, and keeping in general touch with developments. Welfare work for the very young, for the children, is another cause very dear to the Princess. It was no accident that led to the choice of the opening of the new country home at Banstead, Surrey, of the Queen Elizabeth Hospital for Children, Hackney, as the last of her public engagements this summer. The work of that hospital, which caters for the little ones of the back streets of East London, has been of abiding interest to her ever since those distant days when her father and mother used to tell her about the lives of little girls less fortunate than she, after one of their many visits to the three hospitals into which Queen Elizabeth's was then divided.

Cruelty to children is an evil which the Princess abhors. The Royal Society for its prevention has no keener member than its Royal President. This, again, is an old-seated interest of the Princess, and one which commands her most active support. To help such causes efficiently, it is necessary to know rather more than may be gained by a mere reading of reports and appeals, and Princess Elizabeth has no hesitation in taking steps to find out for herself anything she needs to know. An instance of this was her unheralded visit to a London police-court where juvenile cases were being heard by a bench including a woman magistrate. The Princess had heard and read a good deal about juvenile delinquency, and had read, too, criticism of some aspects of the administration of justice to the young. That is a subject she regards as of very great importance, so she went along to see and hear for herself how the law is meted out in daily practice. It was a new world to the Princess as she sat on the bench, under the representation of her father's coat-of-arms which proclaims that it is the King's justice which the magistrates must give. She learned much in the few hours she remained in the court, much, too, from the wise woman magistrate with whom she talked over lunch, but the Princess was not pleased when she heard her visit there, and her visit to the House of Commons as well, described as part of her Royal training and education. That such visits are educative the Princess would certainly not deny, but she regards them as part of the duty of every citizen, of Royal birth or not, who wishes to gain a proper understanding of the society in which he or she lives, and not in any sense a special form of training that is the prerogative of her rank.

It is her desire, as it should be, but rarely is, the desire of all who live in the free democracy of which we are so justly proud, to learn all she can about the way it functions. Visits of a similar kind, therefore, may be expected to form part of the Princess's future programme. She will make them, as far as she is able, in private, without upsetting the normal, regular routine which is, indeed, exactly what she most wants to see, and there will, if her wishes are obeyed, be a complete absence of fuss and ceremonial. Not only the institutions of the State, the Houses of Parliament, the Law Courts (to which she still has, at the time of writing, to make her first visit), nor merely the hospitals and charitable institutions which, traditionally, are the special preserve of interest for Royal ladies, but the docks, the factories, the mines, all parts of the picture of modern life in Britain, are of compelling interest to the lively, aware mind of the Princess. Already she has visited several factories of varying types. Further industrial visits of this kind are certainties for her future. She wants, too, to know more of the way such great institutions as the Bank of England, the Stock Exchange, Lloyd's, and many others, work, and of the part they take in the national life. For her guides in such matters, Princess Elizabeth has at her disposal the best brains in the country, and most of those who have been privileged to show her how one or the other of our great national institutions work have been frankly surprised both at the ready grasp she has of the problems they explain to her, and at the detailed knowledge she has in advance of the background of their work. This all provides yet another instance of Princess Elizabeth's determination to fit herself, by every means she may, for the formidable responsibilities that await her in the future.

Housing, perhaps the most serious of all the problems that are the legacy of war, is another matter of deep concern to the Princess. Suggestions that she should include a call at a new housing estate when she is making an official visit in London or the provinces are apt to meet with a ready response, as when she went to Greenwich to see her husband—himself Baron Greenwich—receive the freedom of the ancient borough. Before the ceremony, the Princess gladly allowed the woman Mayor to show her proudly the new attractively designed blocks of comfortable flats erected by the Council for workers. And the practical nature of the interest she takes in what she sees is illustrated by the fact that the first questions she asked once she had explored a flat and commented on its convenience, were how much was the rent, and how was it related to the weekly wage of the tenants.

Another side of the Princess's life which is of growing importance concerns her position as the first hostess of the younger generation in the Empire. Her official residence, Clarence House, will form, once she and the Duke have taken up residence there, the centre for the young folk of the whole Empire. Her dinner parties, her receptions, will be the meeting grounds for the young men and women from overseas into whose hands the government of the Dominions of the Crown will to-morrow be given. In the loose-woven structure of the British Empire to-day, in which the Crown is the only integral part of the constitution of each separate entity of the Empire common to all, the importance of this personal contact between the young woman who one day will, in all human probability, be called on to rule over it as the wearer of that Crown, and those from whom her own future Ministers are likely to be chosen, cannot be exaggerated. Though she has far too keen an intelligence to find much satisfaction in purely social occasions, the Princess is, as anyone who has had the honour to be her guest well knows, a hostess of singular charm, which is, again, of fortunate advantage for the Empire. Her home, as the pinnacle of Empire hospitality, second only to Buckingham Palace itself, will never be merely a centre for idle entertainment and the interchange of social pleasantries. Such a prospect would be anything but pleasing to the Royal hostess and her husband, both of whom are, for all their love of fun and gay sense of humour, essentially serious-minded folk. Not wealth or rank by birth, but intelligence and honesty of purpose are the qualities by which the Royal couple will judge their guests, and there is much to suggest that the Princess's circle of friends may become as widely and justly famed as the *salons* of the great ladies whose parties were the nucleus of much of the best thought of the day in France of the eighteenth century.

Princess Elizabeth is proud to be the Freeman of more than one great city as well as of several smaller, but equally ancient and honourable boroughs. She holds the Freedom of London, of Edinburgh, and of Cardiff, of Windsor and of Stirling. Still other freedoms of olden British cities and towns, of newer cities and towns in the Dominions await her, together with many other honours of the future. Each honour, indeed, each passing year, will bring additional responsibilities and duties to Princess Elizabeth. The honours she will accept with the same graceful modesty that she has already shown. The responsibilities and duties she will face with the added confidence that her husband is at her side, sharing her ideals and hopes, strengthening her with mutual support and love. Her early indications gave promise of a splendid future. To-day, as that promise begins to be fulfilled, the whole Empire is conscious that however great the occasion, however high the trial, Princess Elizabeth will be equal to it.